Tracks on a Page

Recent Titles in
Women Writers of Color
Joanne M. Braxton, Series Editor

Lucille Clifton: Her Life and Letters
Mary Jane Lupton

June Jordan: Her Life and Letters
Valerie F. Kinloch

Zora Neale Hurston: A Biography of the Spirit
Deborah G. Plant

Border Crossings and Beyond: The Life and Works of Sandra Cisneros
Carmen Haydée Rivera

Nikki Giovanni: A Literary Biography
Virginia C. Fowler

WOMEN WRITERS OF COLOR

Tracks on a Page

Louise Erdrich, Her Life and Works

Frances Washburn

Joanne M. Braxton, Series Editor

 PRAEGER

AN IMPRINT OF ABC-CLIO, LLC
Santa Barbara, California • Denver, Colorado • Oxford, England

Copyright 2013 by Frances Washburn

All rights reserved. No part of this publication may be reproduced, stored in a retrieval system, or transmitted, in any form or by any means, electronic, mechanical, photocopying, recording, or otherwise, except for the inclusion of brief quotations in a review, without prior permission in writing from the publisher.

Library of Congress Cataloging-in-Publication Data

Washburn, Frances.
    Tracks on a Page: Louise Erdrich, her life and works / Frances Washburn.
       pages cm. — (Women Writers of Color)
    Includes bibliographical references and index.
    ISBN 978-0-313-39257-3 (hardcopy : acid-free paper) — ISBN 978-0-313-39258-0
(ebook)   1. Erdrich, Louise.   I. Title.
    PS3555.R42Z94   2013
    813'.54—dc23
    [B]   2013006763

ISBN: 978-0-313-39257-3
EISBN: 978-0-313-39258-0

17 16 15 14 13   1 2 3 4 5

This book is also available on the World Wide Web as an eBook.
Visit www.abc-clio.com for details.

Praeger
An Imprint of ABC-CLIO, LLC

ABC-CLIO, LLC
130 Cremona Drive, P.O. Box 1911
Santa Barbara, California 93116-1911

This book is printed on acid-free paper ∞

Manufactured in the United States of America

To all those wonderful women writers of color, who have shown us the way. Pilamaya ye.

Contents

Series Foreword

The Women Writers of Color Series offers enjoyable reading for an enlightened multi-ethnic audience that includes scholars and critics, poets and writers, librarians and young adults, who read both critically and for entertainment; each volume is published with a user-friendly bibliography so that the readers can pursue original works by these women authors of color and find critical writings more easily.

The Women Writers of Color Series exists for every little girl of any race whoever wrote a poem and hid it, and for every woman writer of color whose work we will never know. This series is therefore not only for the scholar and the critic, but also for the daughters of those mothers whose creativity and intelligence were suppressed or denied—daughters who went on to become poets, essayists, novelists, and activists who inspired others in the creation of artistic models with the vision for a sustainable future.

Native American people, people of color, were here when the first Europeans and Africans arrived in the Americas, living in harmony with the earth; yet, they are underrepresented in the canon of American literature. Among these, Louise Erdrich is both popular and influential, a well-known novelist, poet, memoirist, and author of children's books. The daughter of a German American father and an Ojibwe mother, she grew up in North Dakota and attended Dartmouth College before receiving a Master of Arts degree from Johns Hopkins University. To date, Erdrich has published 14 novels, winning the National Book Critics Circle Award and the Anisfield-Wolf Book Award, among others. A weaver of exquisitely rich narratives, Erdrich portrays the lives of people like those she has known, people who have struggled to retain their lands and their heritage. Her novels often read as if they were being spoken in the present moment; "My girl," she writes, "I have seen the passing of times you will never know." In this way, Erdrich invites her audiences to participate in the creation of meaning by transforming the act of reading into one of healing.

Louise Erdrich's triumph as a Native American and a woman of color writer is cause for celebration. We therefore welcome *Tracks on a Page* by Frances Washburn. Washburn, a novelist and professor of American Indian literature, is at once a scholar and a storyteller. Of Lakota/Irish/German/Anishinaabe heritage, Frances Washburn grew up on the stories of her Irish grandmother and her Lakota grandmother, "historical stories of war and peace, homely stories that conveyed human values and the consequences of behavior, both good and bad." In addition to publishing two novels, Washburn has established her scholarly footing by publishing in *American Indian Quarterly, American Indian Culture and Research Journal, Wicazo Sa,* and *Studies in American Indian Literature.* In *Tracks on a Page,* Washburn follows Louise Erdrich's literary tracks like a seasoned hunter, offering rare insights into a little known journey.

Joanne M. Braxton
College of William and Mary
Series Editor

ONE

The Earth from Which It Springs

L ouise Erdrich's published works are both popular and critically acclaimed—popular in that her books are often on the *New York Times* Best Seller list, an indication that the general public buys large numbers of her books, and critically acclaimed in that her books earn excellent reviews and are often required reading in college literature classes. The combined honor is rare. Popular fiction is often disdained by university literature professors as being writing that appeals to the lowest common denominator. Stephen King's works, for instance, have only recently become acceptable as a topic for literature classes—something that was probably helped when many of his novels, such as *The Green Mile* and *The Shawshank Redemption,* were made into movies that won prestigious awards. Erdrich's works have not been made into movies—not yet—but her work is recognized within popular culture, which makes it all the more remarkable that her books are considered worthy of literature status because of the mistaken assumption by many critics and academic scholars that what is popular cannot also be good. Popular fiction is assumed to be fleeting in value, the whim of a finite moment in time, while literature is defined as those works that have something of value to impart that will stand the test of time.

That Erdrich's work is also considered Native American literature, rather than popular fiction with Indian characters and themes, is partly because there are very few Native Americans who are writing fiction, or for that matter have ever published anything at all, which means that there is a limited choice for any college literature course that concentrates on Native American literature. However, that fact in no way diminishes the quality of Erdrich's work.

Native American literature is one category in the ethnic literatures genre introduced into college curriculums since the tumultuous 1960s era of the civil rights movements and the concomitant recognition that the United States is made up of many ethnic minorities that include people of African American, American Indian, Asian, Latino/a, and Middle Eastern origin, and many other people of color. These groups have stories to tell that are different from those of mainstream White America, but are just as interesting, just as well-written, and worthy of notice as literature that has roots in Europe. The best way to learn about another culture is to learn their language, but if that is not possible or practical, then learn their stories.

Prior to the 1960s, much had been written about American Indians, but very little had been written *by* them, and those few works were almost always written in collaboration with a White author or mediated by a White editor. Further, much of this published work was cultural or historical— anthropological content from an insider's perspective.

In the early 20th century, anthropologists such as Franz Boas, and later Claude Levi-Strauss, rushed to remote Indian communities to chronicle their culture and language in the mistaken belief that Indians were vanishing, dying off, and that a body of interesting information would die with them. Of course, that did not happen. The American Indian population in this country has grown, and while there are major challenges for many American Indian communities, they—and their cultures and stories—are nowhere near extinction.

Much of what was written about Indians by non-native authors was distinctly patronizing, at best, or demeaning and dehumanizing, at worst. Frequently, such literature dismissed Native American cultural perspectives that were different from those of mainstream Euro-American positions and beliefs, as Louis Owens wrote, "like James Fenimore Cooper's Natty Bumpo dismissing a Pawnee description of heaven with his own privileged European version."[1] Early authors writing about Indians failed to recognize or willfully ignored the fact that White colonists had invaded and taken possession of American Indian land and natural resources, brought European diseases that killed upward of 90 percent of the native population, and did not seem to understand why Indians would take offense at those actions. These Euro-American-authored books set up binaries of good Indians and bad Indians, noble Red Men and savage Red Men. Often, plots involved White settlers who had moved onto native land and were about to be attacked by the Indians they were displacing. The attacking Indians were portrayed as the savages, but often, one Indian, usually a child, warned the settlers and saved them, thus becoming the noble Red Man. Further, Indians who foreswore their own traditional spiritual practices to become Christians were noble; those who rejected Christianity were savages.

Euro-American citizens in the early United States were fond of stories that detailed the Christian conversion of American Indians, and for some, it may have been because religion, bringing the "truth" to the unenlightened savages, was a justification for what amounted to a massive land grab and genocide. Other citizens of the United States, if not most, probably never thought much about the early history of the country, other than that it was founded on the principles of religious freedom and "all men are created equal," which were true only if the person speaking of such freedoms was male, heterosexual, and White. Films perpetrated the image of American Indians as savages, sometimes noble, but usually not, particularly in the westerns directed and produced by John Ford and starring John Wayne, where the White settlers or soldiers were the good guys and the Indians were screaming savages bent on destroying all that was Christian and fine. Perhaps the most egregious of these films is *The Searchers,* wherein a White settler community is attacked by Indians and all the White members are killed except for two little girls, who are taken captive. The uncle of the girls, played by John Wayne, spends years searching the west for his nieces, not to rescue them, but to kill them because they have been contaminated by living with savages.

Later fiction about American Indians romanticized their culture and the Indian people. Indians were not savage but noble, possessing a spiritual connection, especially to land and to animals, that was not available to non-Native Americans. While the decades of the 1960s and the 1970s called attention to racial, ethnic, and gender inequalities, in the case of American Indians, people and movements of the era also brought nostalgia for something exotic and different that never existed. Young people and some not-so-young wore beads and fringe, turquoise and silver, and discovered that at least one of their ancestors was an Indian, usually Cherokee, the one tribe that most non-Native Americans had heard of. To be fair, some people really did have a native person or two in their family tree, but while they may have been genuinely proud of that, few knew what being a Cherokee, or any other tribe of Indians really meant, historically or culturally.

Owens wrote, "The fact that, as D.H. Lawrence clearly recognized, at the heart of America's history of Indian hating is an unmistakable yearning to *be* Indian—romantically and from a distance made hazy through fear and guilt—compounds the complexity."[2] At the beginning of the 21st century, the pendulum swings of interest from Indian hating to Indian desire seem to have reached a point of near equilibrium. The accepting, even embracing of ethnic cultures that prevailed in the 1960s and 1970s has subsided as conservative politics have gained momentum and ethnocentrisms in the form of anti-immigration movements come to the fore. American Indians, who make up less than 1 percent of the population in the United States, have become invisible for much of the mainstream Euro-American population for many reasons.

Physically, American Indians differ widely in appearance. There is no typical physiognomy, even though many uninformed people think of Indians as being medium to tall in height with dark skin, dark brown or black eyes and hair, a prominent nose and high cheekbones. Some Indians do look like that, but Indians come in all shapes and sizes, with variations in hair and eye color. All of this means that Indians blend in with other populations, which contributes to their invisibility. Indians who do have dark skin, hair, and eyes may be mistaken for Middle Eastern, South Asian or Latino, while fair-skinned Indians with light eyes may be assumed to be of European origin. Further, Indians do not necessarily have exotic-sounding names such as Big Eagle or Black Horse, but often have names that were assigned to them in the historical past by White missionaries in boarding schools or by soldiers at forts, or that were acquired when a distant ancestor married a French explorer or fur trapper, as is common with many characters in Erdrich's works. Further, as the population in the United States has shifted, becoming less White and more brown, there has been a reaction by some conservative citizens who are afraid that "White" culture is being subsumed beneath a rising tide of "Other."

Writers of color provide a counterweight to that fear by demonstrating through characters in their stories that brown "Others" are human beings with the same hopes, fears, and dreams as mainstream people of European descent. Poverty, sickness, divorce, and all the other ills that beset mankind are color-blind, as are the desires to love and be loved, a stable income, a healthy body, and a satisfying career. Of all the ethnic literatures, however, American Indian literature may be the hardest to understand, and the easiest to overlook or ignore.

The economic situations of universities and colleges means, among other woes, that administrators choose course topics that will enroll the most students, and for Ethnic Studies departments or English departments, that often means the demand is for African American literature or, increasingly, Latino/a literature because those populations are higher than that of American Indians. A few intrepid souls want to explore beyond the literatures of the most numerous minorities, so there are American Indian literature (or, as more commonly labeled, Native American literature) classes, but often, American Indian literature is included as an "also ran" in an umbrella class that offers literature from many ethnic groups. When the money is divided up for special events in an Ethnic Studies department at a university or college, it usually goes to pay fees for African American or Latino/a speakers and projects rather than American Indians. Without the demand from students, as happened in the early 1970s at San Francisco State University, the University of California at Berkeley, and other institutions of higher education, American Indian literature is easily overlooked.

Of all the ethnic literatures, that of American Indians is the most exotic, and the most difficult to understand in any depth. Any American student or citizen can read standard, mainstream American writing by an American author without any great difficulty because there is a shared culture in which everyone participates. At the base of this culture is the meta-narrative of Christian-Judeo religious practice and of capitalism as a political and social system. When an author writes that a character goes to church, the reader immediately understands the physical act of attending a church service, but also assumes that the church is Christian (or secondarily, Jewish), and the author assumes that the reader has at least a rudimentary knowledge of Christian belief and practice.

When an author creates a character who works and earns a salary from which taxes are withheld, then spends that paycheck for living expenses or to buy other things—needful or not—the reader understands, without even thinking about it, that the character is participating in a capitalist economy.

African American literature includes universal themes of love, hate, poverty, loss, and desire, among a myriad of other themes, but in African American literature, these themes are influenced by the history of slavery and its aftermath—racism and oppression. Of course, that makes it very different from mainstream American literature, but Africans brought to the Americas were brutally stripped of most culture and religious practice, indoctrinated and Christianized to such a depth that, generally speaking, only remnants of their original culture and spiritual practice remain intact. Mainstream television programs such as the mini-series *Roots,* based on the books by Alex Haley, encouraged many African Americans to search for their own ancestral origins in Africa and to recover their traditional cultural and spiritual practices.

African American English may differ, in some cases markedly, from standard American English, but it is understandable to any English speaker, with little need for explanation and translation. In the main, Christianity and capitalism are still bound into the stories and plots of African American literature, making it accessible for other reading audiences.

The same is true, and perhaps more so, of Latino/a American literature. People of Latino heritage have a history of interaction with Christianity and capitalism going back to their roots in Spain, introduced by Spanish colonizers and forced, often upon pain of death, upon their American Indian subjects, and carried on to the mixed blood descendants. Cultural differences in Latino/a literature involve both cultural practice and linguistic expression, but when a book is written in English with a few Spanish words here and there, most of those words are discernible from the context, making that work still accessible to mainstream readers.

Asian American literature, whether the characters and plots are of Japanese, Chinese, South Asian (India or Pakistan) or some other Asian origin, is less comprehensible because that meta-narrative of Christianity and capitalism is not always present. The spiritual practice invoked in those stories may be Buddhist or Hindu, Taoist, Islamic, or partake of any of dozens, possibly hundreds, of cultural practices and belief systems. Social organizational systems are not necessarily capitalism, but may be some form of socialism, communalism, or feudalism. But Asian American literature, particularly contemporary, still partakes of western capitalism culture. Indeed, the Japanese have become so good at capitalism/business practices that some Americans, up until the recent natural and economic disasters, were afraid that Japan would surpass the United States economically. The decade of the 1980s was rife with rumors, innuendo, and fearmongering conspiracy stories of everyone in the United States being required to learn Japanese within 10 years because the Japanese were coming to take over the United States. Asian people have also become Christian converts in large numbers, and some, particularly under British colonization in India and China, have been Christian for generations.

American Indian literature is the most difficult of all to understand, particularly if a story is set in the historical past, pre-colonial contact. There are over 500 different federally recognized tribes or nations of American Indians within the United States and more than 100 tribes that have been recognized by individual states, and each of those tribes has a different language, culture, spiritual practice, and geographical location, which are factors in works published by their respective tribal members. Some mainstream readers assume that all American Indians speak the same language and partake of the same culture. Certainly, some tribes who live in proximity to each other do share cultural and spiritual practices and a few words and verbal expressions, but in general, each tribe is a distinct entity, and their cultural and spiritual practices make their stories very different. In addition, traditional Indian society was not organized under the capitalist system, but rather, through a kinship system. Each person belonged to an extended family, with obligations to each other and expectations of reciprocity that worked very well to ensure no person starved while others were wealthy; that system provided for children, the sick, and the elderly and meted out punishments to wrongdoers. While contemporary American Indians live in and partake of the mainstream capitalist society, there are also remnants of the kinship system that still exist and function in American Indian daily lives for most tribes. In spite of the best efforts of Christians to eradicate all traces of native spiritual practice, most tribes still maintain aspects of their own specific notions of what is god, if there is more than one, what role those gods might play in the lives of people and so on, and maintain specific ceremonies that honor their gods or ask for assistance or advice in solving problems. These tribally specific epistemologies are a part of Native American storytelling.

All of these differences are woven into the fabric of American Indian literature, and what differences are depicted depend upon the tribal identity not only of the author, but of the characters portrayed in the stories. A Lakota writer may tell a story of lost love that is completely different from that of a story of lost love written by an Ojibwe writer, and both will be very much different from a story on the same theme written by a mainstream American author. A mainstream reader who is uninformed of the culture, language, and spiritual practice described in an American Indian novel is likely to completely misunderstand the context or to simply give up and put the book aside. As Karl Kroeber has written, Native American novels are "not so accessible; and most create doubts, difficulties, and frustrations for a serious reader trying to understand in depth, wishing to gain something more than a superficial, and therefore patronizing, 'appreciation' of Native American literary art."[3]

Storytelling is a central part of traditional American Indian culture, in part because in nonliterate societies, all information must be remembered. Words become sacred because to forget important facts, about weather, for example, might have meant the death of an entire group of people, and putting important survival information into story form makes that information easier to remember. Putting that story into a song with rhythm makes the story even more memorable, which is true of all human beings, not just American Indians.

To demonstrate that, think of how many children in kindergarten are taught the alphabet. They learn the ABC song, and even adults 60 years of age or more still remember that song. Children are also taught stories such as Little Red Riding Hood, which are not just for entertainment; they are also didactic. Little Red Riding Hood can have several important lessons, such as "beware of strangers," or more specifically, "don't open the door to strangers." While modern mainstream stories—even movies and stage plays and songs—may be considered as only entertainment, there are messages in almost everything, even if it is one of the oldest ones—beware of strangers. While storytelling as a survival mechanism was important in the past, it is still considered valuable in contemporary times, as Native American writer Leslie Marmon Silko wrote:

> I will tell you something about stories,
> [he said]
> They aren't just entertainment.
> Don't be fooled.
> They are all we have, you see,
> all we have to fight off
> illness and death.[4]

The literature of every culture in the world has its roots in stories of oral tradition that were also told for purposes that were not "just entertainment." Print culture, and consequently, widespread literacy, has only been around since the invention of the printing press around 1440, and even so, it has taken many years, centuries even, for literacy to become common. However, in countries where literacy is commonplace and books are ubiquitous, readers have come to have certain expectations from written stories, such as a chronological ordering of the story that makes the plot easily understood. Any flashbacks are clearly signaled by the author so the reader knows when a section is something that took place in the past. Generally speaking, plots of mainstream novels progress in a linear fashion from A to B to C to D, and so on. Except in rare cases where time travel is a feature of the plot, time in Euro-western stories is unidirectional from the past to the present to the future. However, time in American Indian traditional thought is neither linear nor unidirectional, but cyclical. The seasons follow in order, but are repeated every year with all the natural events that take place in each season, which coincide with ceremonial practice. Likewise, American Indian literature honors that sense of time as a circle with the potential for movement backward as well as forward. The plots of mainstream novels move like a train down a track toward a destination, with other sub-plots or tracks that branch off from each side, but eventually loop back into the main track until, at the end, the story/train arrives at the final destination. The story is contained within this neatly complete structure.

However, American Indian stories, and Erdrich's, follow this pattern more often than not, resemble trees that have a central plot or branch, but other branches or twigs that burst off from that main trunk and do not loop back, but grow out in all directions, not merely forward or up. Below ground, roots move downward and outward in a mirror image of what is seen above ground, so a story may move upward and outward in any direction, but also downward and outward in multiple directions. The point is not to arrive at a destination or end with a set understanding, but to create the possibility for multiple readings or multiple interpretations of meaning.

Consistency in verb tenses in mainstream literature is important to anchor a story in time, whether that is past, present, or rarely, future, even though the average reader is unlikely to notice this aspect. However, as E. Shelley Reid points out, the verb tenses in Erdrich's writing slip backward and forward. Reid writes that "the narrative whips through time as though chronological distinctions never existed."[5] A quote from a chapter in *Love Medicine* illustrates this technique:

> "Some men react in that situation [the strip poker game Lulu played with Beverly and his brother Henry twenty years earlier] and some don't," she told him. "It was reaction I looked for, if you know what I mean." [*past events*] Beverley was silent.
>
> Lulu winked at him . . . At the time [*present*] she would burn it off when her house caught fire, and it would never [*far future*] grow back. Because her face was soft and yet alert [*present*], . . . Beverly had always [*past*] felt exposed, preyed on, undressed around her, even before the game in which she'd stripped him naked [*past*] and now [*present*], as he found, appraised him in his shame.[6]

The linear nature of time in mainstream written work is the norm, but stories told orally, no matter the culture of origination, do not necessarily follow that pattern. Human beings are still oral; we tell stories to each other. We do not write notes and pass them. When we are telling friends about a trip to the store, it is likely to be out of sequence because humans forget things and have to go back and insert more information to make meaning clear, or add information at the end to explain why the trip to the store ended the way it did, or why it was important. Societies that have more recently become literate often still use oral storytelling techniques within their written literature, while societies with a longer history of literacy have gotten out of the habit of understanding written stories that are not told in a linear fashion.

The closer in time that a society is to exclusive orality rather than literacy, the more those elements of oral tradition appear in texts written by members of that society. Besides a nonlinear plot, other elements might include repetition, flash-forwards as well as flashbacks, rhyming words, and the use of the second person narrative.

Repetition is an important element in societies that are nonliterate because it is an aid to memory, and if there are no written records of useful or necessary information, then everything must be archived within human memory.

In stories, the important information may be only one line. It may also be that the entire story contains multiple bits of information, and in some cases, the story may be told by more than one person, with each person repeating the same information in different ways. Erdrich utilizes this technique in many of her novels and notably so in *Tracks,* where the characters of Pauline and Nanapush alternately tell the story. Each of these storytellers has a different version of how they perceive other characters and events within the story, even though each has a bit more information than the other about a particular character or event. This technique allows Erdrich to give a more complete picture of any particular event or character than if only one person was narrating; however, the dual (or perhaps "duel" because Pauline and Nanapush comment upon each other) narration presents another dilemma for the reader—when the information given by each of the narrators conflicts, who should the reader believe? Which one is telling the truth, which is lying, or is there no truth but only individual perception? Erdrich casts both Pauline and Nanapush as sympathetic characters when they are first introduced, but as the story progresses, Pauline's words begin to contradict her earlier statements like a criminal tripped up on the witness stand by their own lies, and further, she seems oblivious to her own deceptions. Or possibly, she is aware and is manipulating the reader, or rather, Erdrich is manipulating the reader through her characters. It is easy to forget that Pauline and Nanapush are not real living humans, but creations from Erdrich's imagination. The ability to make characters come alive and walk off the page is the sign of a master storyteller. Nanapush is just as much of a manipulator as is Pauline, but the difference is that Nanapush never lies to himself, never pretends that he is not a trickster. In the end, most readers decide that Nanapush is the reliable narrator, but there is always room for doubt. This dual/duel narration undermines the Euro-western expectation that at the heart of every story, there is a single truth, while following the repetition element so common in oral tradition.

While Nanapush and Pauline tell conflicting truths about the same stories, nevertheless, they are both members of the same community, and as such, each of them possesses the right to tell stories as they perceive them or as they wish others to perceive them. They are illustrating the collective identity of their community, as Pauline Reid pointed out in her article when she argued that the technique of utilizing multiple narrators indicates a collectiveness of identity. She insists, too, that the repetition of the same story told from multiple viewpoints indicates an overall identity that goes beyond the individual characters. People who recognize and iterate a shared history through stories are more likely to work together as a group to survive, and even overcome, adversity. In *Tracks,* Pauline desperately wants to deny her heritage and trade her Indian community for a White one, but the stories she tells about herself and her community deny that possibility. Nanapush chooses to embrace his Indian heritage and community, and his storytelling anchors him within both, and even, against her own wishes, ties Pauline to Nanapush and the community.

Not always these days, but still enough to be notable, American Indian literature utilizes elements of orality that make it more difficult to understand for the reader used to the Euro-American narrative structure of writing. All of the above—stories drawing from cultures that are not rooted in Judeo-Christian spiritual practice or capitalist society, a multiplicity of languages and cultures, and closer historical ties to orality rather than literacy—make American Indian literature uniquely different and difficult to understand for the Euro-American reader. Yet, remarkably, Louise Erdrich's work is more widely read and appreciated than that of many mainstream American writers. Why?

Erdrich's themes and plots are universal—love, illness, poverty, and death—and resonate with readers of any culture, which is a reason they have appeal for the mass-market audience. The details with which she surrounds these stories, the characters and their unique positioning as American Indian citizens of particular native nations in general, and Ojibwe in specific, are not only part of who Erdrich is as a human being and a writer, but offer enough of the exotic and different to fascinate mainstream readers looking for something outside the usual. Her work can be read without any knowledge of American Indian literature in general or of Ojibwe stories and culture in specific. However, for an American Indian reader, her stories take on a depth that harks to their own experience, or perhaps, the experience of an Indian relative or friend, and the result is an echoing of verisimilitude not found in most published works that are simply *about* Indians rather than *by* Indians.

The first paragraph of her novel, *Tracks,* is a masterpiece of writing, both in craft that anyone, Indian or not, can understand, but is also a manifesto that proclaims this writer is an American Indian, and specifically, a Chippewa person who understands the history and culture of Indian people within the colonial and postcolonial context of the United States. It is useful to include that entire section here:

> We started dying before the snow, and like the snow, we continued to fall. It was surprising there were so many of us left to die. For those who survived the spotted sickness from the south, our long fight west to Nadouissioux land where we signed the treaty, and then a wind from the east, bringing exile in a storm of government papers, what descended from the north in 1912 seemed impossible.[7]

From a craft standpoint, the beginning sentence is masterful. It contains a hook that pulls the reader into the story. This opening simile that compares dying people to falling snow is unique, creating a picture in the readers' minds. The rest of the paragraph continues to pique a reader's curiosity with the implication that this "we" has overcome other disasters, and the information is given in a flowing sentence that leads the reader on in a most Faulkner-like style. But, for an American Indian and especially for an Indian of the Chippewa tribe, this paragraph is packed full of information that they know, either from personal experience or family or tribal history.

Some non-Indian readers may not know from the scanty information contained in K-12 history books or from personal reading that European diseases
to which Indigenous Americans had no natural immunity killed more Indians
than did the guns of White settlers and inter-tribal warfare, but Indians are well
aware of this fact. As European White settlers arrived in the Americas, they
brought with them infectious diseases that were not necessarily fatal to the Europeans, but were deadly to the Indians. One contact between one European
who might not even have felt sick and one Indigenous person could easily
have spread that deadly illness throughout entire families, tribes, and eventually regions, and in actuality, there many such contacts. Disease raced ahead
of the settlers, killing Indians as it went. Some of the diseases that may have
been agents of death include small pox, cholera, bubonic plague, and even ordinary childhood diseases such as chicken pox and mumps. Erdrich refers to
the "spotted sickness," but this was a catchall term used by many Indians and
could have referred to any disease that produced a rash or pustules.

An uninformed reader might notice that Erdrich writes of difficulties coming from south, west, east, and north, and see those words as simply a poetic
convention, but Indians know that Erdrich is referencing the four sacred directions, which are inevitably called upon when engaging in spiritual performance and ceremonies. The difficulties coming from each of these directions
also refer to incidents in Indian history, such as the already mentioned spotted
sickness coming from the south.

The next part of the sentence, "the long fight west to Nadouissioux land," is
a specific reference to Chippewa people, whose original homeland was much
farther to the east, but who were pushed farther and farther west by White colonization until they ended up in what was the territory of the Sioux tribe. The
word Nadouissioux comes from the Anishinabe word Nadowe-is-iw,[8] which
translates to lesser adder (snake), another term for enemy. French fur trappers
in the region changed the word to Nadouissioux, but eventually the word was
shortened to simply, Sioux, which is the term for a group of Northern Plains
tribes, who often refer to themselves now as Lakota, Dakota, or Nakota.

The next section, "bringing exile in a storm of government papers," is more
nebulous, but Erdrich is probably referring to Federal Indian Law and Policy,
which includes court cases and federal legislation that effectively treated Indians as children, wards of the government, with little agency. The last part of
the sentence, "what descended from the north in 1912 seemed impossible," is
about yet another wave of infectious disease, as Erdrich describes in the following chapter and at other places in the book. This disease is not defined, and
the symptoms could be any of many that afflicted native people, but it may
have been the forerunner of the influenza pandemic that would kill thousands
of people around the world during World War I.

Any reader, mainstream Euro-American or American Indian, can appreciate
this section, but obviously, the more informed the reader, the more that reader
will understand and appreciate American Indian literature, and especially the

works of Louise Erdrich. Every author brings personal experience and culture to their work, even if it is only in the patterns of language they use. Erdrich's personal experience and cultural heritage is German American on her father's side and Turtle Mountain Chippewa on her mother's side of the family. Her writing draws upon both.

Her German American grandparents owned and ran a butcher shop, and Erdrich's knowledge of that business is a part of several of her novels, including *Tracks* and *The Master Butcher's Singing Club.* In *Tracks,* much of the information included is historical, such as the details about how meat was preserved in times before refrigeration became common—in a cave lined with blocks of ice cut from the river in winter. These details may not be common knowledge for every reader, but Erdrich makes them understandable for any reader, even modern ones who are so accustomed to refrigerators that any prior idea about food preservation is noticeable by its absence.

What is less understandable for uninformed readers are the Chippewa history, culture, and spiritual belief and practice that are everywhere included in Erdrich's work. An encyclopedic knowledge of the Ojibwe people is not necessary to understand the roots of Erdich's life and works, but some basic information is helpful to understanding nuances within the stories.

The Chippewa people are also known as the Ojibwa, Ojibwe, or Ojibway, and they are part of the larger group known as the Anishinaabe or Anishinabe, which includes Algonquin, Nipissing, Oji-Cree, Odawa, and the Potawatomi. Originally, their home territory surrounded the Great Lakes on both sides of what is now the Canadian and U.S. borders from as far east as New York and as far west as northeastern North Dakota and all of southern Canada between these two points. The encroachment of White settlers on their territory pushed them farther west and their homelands now stretch from Michigan to Montana, and the corresponding Canadian lands north of those U.S. states.

There are more than 50 branches of the Ojibwe people, called First Nations or Bands in Canada, and sometimes called Bands in the United States. Erdrich is a member of the Turtle Mountain Band of Chippewa Indians, and most of her works reference that particular band.[9] Their reservation is located in north central North Dakota, very close to the Canadian border, while Wahpeton, where Erdrich grew up, is located in the southeastern corner of the state on the North Dakota and Minnesota state line. When the Ojibwe people were forced to migrate from the Eastern Great Lakes area to their present location, they moved into territory already occupied by branches of the Sioux Nation. Conflicts took place between these different groups, but at the present time, both tribal nations have reservations in North Dakota and South Dakota and many members of both groups live off reservation in rural areas and small towns. As is always true when cultures live in proximity to one another, a pattern usually develops. First, there is conflict, then an uneasy truce, then acceptance, and eventually, inter-marriages until each culture adopts some aspects of the other in language, culture, and spiritual practice, while retaining their own essential unique aspects.

One such spiritual performance that Erdrich details in many of her works is the sweat lodge ceremony, which is practiced by Ojibwe, Dakota (Sioux), and other Native American groups, not only in the upper Midwest, but increasingly across the United States and Canada. This ceremony may be performed for many different reasons—as an offering of thanks to spirits for a favor or boon granted, to seek guidance for a current difficulty, or any of many other purposes. Generally, hot rocks are heated and placed inside a windowless covered structure. Participants gather inside, sitting in a circle while water is periodically poured on the rocks creating steam. Prayers or pleas or thanks are offered by individual participants in a set formula, usually proceeding around the circle in a counter clockwise direction. At the conclusion of the ceremony, participants usually bathe in cold water and eat a meal together. However, one uniquely Ojibwe belief involves the *windigo* spirit.

The *windigo*, sometimes spelled *wendigo*, is a common figure in Ojibwe stories and in Erdrich's work. The *windigo* is a monstrous cannibal that appears as a result of human greed, envy, and jealousy, usually in winter when the Ojibwe people are often suffering from starvation and cold. Julie Tharp writes about Erdrich's use of the *windigo* as a character in her novel, *The Antelope Wife.*[10] According to Tharp:

> Erdrich presents a strong case for the relevance of Ojibwe philosophy to present-day mainstream U.S. culture. The central theme of eating and food, the setting of Gakahbekong or modern-day Minneapolis, and the presence of windigo characters, all contribute to a meditation on the social ills of overconsumption.[11]

Using her own personal cultural background in Ojibwe history and culture, Erdrich breaks down the binaries of noble versus savage, good versus evil, us versus them, to show the readers a glimpse of native people who live within the double cultural setting that is both American Indian/Ojibwe and Euro-western. The Ojibwe people and the non-native characters within her stories all share a basic humanity. A Neil Diamond song from 1970 illustrates this point quite clearly. In the song, Diamond sings what seems like a simple list of people's names, famous and infamous, but the last stanza makes the meaning clear when Diamond sings that all the people he has just named have one thing in common—they were all human beings who lived and worked and wondered, and wept when their lives were over "For being done too soon."[12]

NOTES

1. Louis Owens, *Other Destinies: Understanding the American Indian Novel* (Norman: University of Oklahoma Press, 1992), 8.

2. Ibid., 3.

3. Karl Kroeber, ed., *Traditional Literatures of the American Indian: Texts and Interpretations* (Lincoln: University of Nebraska Press, 1981). Qtd. in Louise Owens, *Other Destinies,* 15.

4. Leslie Marmon Silko, *Ceremony* (New York: Penguin Books, 1977), 2.

5. E. Shelley Reid, "The Stories We Tell: Louise Erdrich's Identity Narratives," *MELUS* 25:3/4, Traditions Double Issue (Autumn–Winter 2000): 74.

6. Louise Erdrich, *Love Medicine* (New York: Harper Collins, 1993), 116.

7. Louise Erdrich, *Tracks* (New York: HarperCollins First Perennial Library Edition, 1989), 1.

8. Free Resources: Fall 2008 "History and the Headlines," Collections from ABC-CLIO, www.historyandtheheadlines.abcclio.com.

9. For more information on the Turtle Mountain Band of Chippewa Indians, see their website at http:/tmbci.net/wordpress.

10. Louise Erdrich, *The Antelope Wife* (New York: Harper Perennial, 2009).

11. Julie Tharp, "Windigo Ways: Eating and Excess in Louise Erdrich's *The Antelope Wife*," *American Indian Culture and Research Journal* 27:4 (2003): 117–131.

12. Neil Diamond, "Done Too Soon," Prophet Music, Inc., 1970.

TWO

Seeds and Sprouts

Always an adventurous man, at the age of 17, Ralph Louis Erdrich worked his way through Alaska, earning his living by playing poker and by working as a cook's helper. He sent home some of the money to help out his parents, who owned and operated a butcher shop in Wahpeton, North Dakota. The family had also lived in Little Falls, Long Prairie, and Elmore, Minnesota. After service in the Air Force, Ralph went to school on the GI Bill, earned teaching credentials and set off on a new adventure—teaching American Indian students on the Turtle Mountain Chippewa Indian Reservation in North Dakota. Here, he met tribal chairman Patrick Gourneau.[1]

An able storyteller and talker, Gourneau and Erdrich became friends. Of course, Gourneau's handsome young daughter, Rita Joane, was an incentive for Ralph Erdrich to make continuous and numerous visits to the Gourneau home. At that time, Rita was attending the State School of Service in Wahpeton. The two were married by Father George at Saint Ann's Church in Belcourt, North Dakota. Karen Louise Erdrich, the first child of Ralph and Rita Gourneau Erdrich, arrived at Saint Mary's Hospital in Little Falls, Minnesota, on June 7, 1954.

The 1950s era into which Erdrich was born was both a hopeful time and a turbulent time in the United States. Post–World War II, the economy was growing; former servicemen home from the war and anxious to get on with their lives usually married and had children, who comprised the biggest population bubble in American history—the baby boomers. There were opportunities to be had in the cities of Michigan, Ohio, Illinois, and Indiana, where the auto industry grew rapidly as young families bought their first cars on the time payment plan. Young men in the Midwest and the South and elsewhere took over family farms and bought modern innovations in equipment and farming practices. Movies starring the likes of Elizabeth Taylor, Rock Hudson, and Debbie Reynolds thrilled people at the drive-in theaters and shocked people with their rumored risqué lifestyles off-screen. As Americans became more prosperous, many buying homes for the first time, a dark undercurrent also pervaded the country.

Beginning in 1950, Sen. Joseph McCarthy of Wisconsin publicly accused well-known Americans of being communist sympathizers. It was the era of the Red scare as Russian power and influence in the world grew. Some of the very people that Americans admired in the movie theaters were accused of being communist sympathizers, as were members of President Harry Truman's administration and high-placed officials in the U.S. Army.

In 1954, the year of Erdrich's birth, the United States held the McCarthy hearings, ostensibly to investigate the private lives of Americans accused of being members of the Communist Party. However, the hearings did not go as McCarthy would have wished. The country soon became tired of the witch hunt, and when McCarthy and his committee could produce no evidence to support their claims against ordinary Americans, McCarthy found himself discredited. He was censured by the Senate in 1954 and died only three years later, at the age of 48, most likely from complications of alcoholism. For most Americans, the fear of a communist under every bed receded like the memory of a bad dream. But, for American Indians, particularly the Turtle Mountain Chippewa Indians of Erdrich's family, a long nightmare was only beginning.

In 1943, a survey conducted by the U.S. Senate concluded that living conditions on reservations were extremely poor, and that serious mismanagement by the Bureau of Indian Affairs (BIA) was the root cause of this endemic poverty. Congress decided that the solution was neither reform of the BIA nor further investment in education and infrastructure and job creating programs, but rather, the termination of the special relationship between the tribes and the federal government. Goals of this termination policy included ending federal supervision of tribes by abolishing the BIA and repealing discriminatory laws against Indians. While these lofty goals may have sounded good in theory, in practice, termination also meant the immediate withdrawal of any government assistance in the form of federal aid and services as well as removal of all Indian land from trust status, which made the land vulnerable to alienation from its Indian owners by unscrupulous people. Furthermore, all Indian tribes, which were sovereign nations with their own laws, policies, and practices under treaty agreements going back for hundreds of years, would suddenly be subject to the laws of whatever state within which the tribe was located.

No doubt, some people in positions of power saw these moves as beneficial to American Indians since, theoretically at least, they would be brought into mainstream society, but there was another, far less, philanthropic reason for this action. The U.S. government after World War II was deeply in debt. Terminating the relationship with Indian tribes would also mean ending its financial obligation to them, thus saving the United States a considerable amount of money—never mind that doing so would violate treaty obligations. It took 10 years before this policy was actually enabled in 1953 with the first of several Senate and House bills, which eventually resulted in the House Concurrent Resolution 108. This bill called for immediate termination of the Turtle Mountain Chippewa Tribe, along with four other specifically named tribes,[2] and all tribes in California, New York, Florida, and Texas. This was not the equivalent of throwing a wealthy socialite out of a penthouse apartment. American Indians then, as now, were among the poorest of the poor in the United States. Suddenly removing all support—whether in the form of commodity food through the U.S. Dept. of Agriculture, health care, or minimal cash payments—would have had devastating results. Further, removing all American Indian lands from trust status would immediately open the Indians to predatory land grabs. Indeed, at least some of the land owned and occupied by tribes was valuable for the natural resources present in the form of timber, fisheries, coal, oil, natural gas, and uranium deposits. Finally, the move was a violation of the sovereignty of native nations guaranteed by treaties.

The fight against termination would continue for 20 years, with Erdrich's maternal grandfather as Tribal Council President of the Turtle Mountain Chippewa guiding his tribe through this troublesome and frightening time. This situation would no doubt have been a topic of conversation at family gatherings for Erdrich as she grew up and would have shaped her view of Indian–White relationships and her own place in both the world of the Turtle Mountain Chippewa and the wider world of mainstream society.

Wahpeton, North Dakota, where Erdrich was raised surrounded by her family and siblings, is a small town just across the Missouri River from its twin town of Breckenridge, Minnesota. People here are a hardy folk, surviving as they must the harsh blasts of winter blizzards blustering across the plains, the violent summer storms that sometimes spawn tornadoes, and spring floods that threaten to overtop the levies built to protect the communities from the rising water of the river that flows between Wahpeton and Breckenridge. In and around Wahpeton, women were still mostly stay-at-home wives and mothers who looked after their children and cleaned their neat brick or wood frame houses while their husbands ran the local drugstore, clerked in the hardware store, or farmed the rich prairie soil and worried about their crops. Everyone watched the skies for the vicious summer storms that could wipe out a farmer's fields in less than five minutes or the winter blizzards that could claim many of the rancher's newly born and vulnerable calves. Of course, the prosperity of the farmers influenced the prosperity of the town shopkeepers. People lived close to the earth and directly or indirectly depended on it for their livelihood. The local population hunted deer, pheasant, grouse, ducks, and geese in season and out to supplement the family dinner menu.

The town was, and still is, a Beaver Cleaver kind of place where people go to church on Sundays, honor their war veterans, cheer for their high school sports teams, and celebrate many holidays with a parade down Main Street. The majority of the population is of Euro-American descent, mostly German or Norwegian, with some claiming Irish or French or English ancestry. Brown folks are not very numerous, but there are a few African Americans and, of course, Indians of Ojibwe and Lakota and mixed tribal heritages. Back in the 1950s and 1960s, Erdrich would have been unusual with her bi-ethnic heritage, but she seems to have no painful memories of being different or ostracized because of it. Indeed, an essay she wrote for *Smithsonian* magazine is a tribute to her hometown. She begins the essay by stating that early in her life, like young people in small towns everywhere, she had wanted to escape from the insularity of the place. That comment probably indicates the desire for adventure, for evading the seeming emptiness of small town life that many teenagers experience. However, Erdrich continues that in spite of those teenage yearnings for escape, in her later years, her hometown is a place that, ". . . [I] have ever after held close in my heart,"[3] a sentiment that seems to be an echo of many other adventure-seeking young people who left their hometowns for the wider world, but returned in middle age or old age for a visit or even to retire, realizing that the peacefulness and security of small town America was not a bad place to start, and perhaps to end, a life.

Unlike many towns where the streets wander in odd jogs and loops to follow the topography of the landscape, Wahpeton is laid out in regular squares with straight streets, which in many places used to be lined with big elm trees. Unfortunately, Dutch elm disease claimed most of these giant beauties in the 1960s. Buildings, too, have fallen into disrepair, some demolished to make way for newer ones, and others put to different uses. In her *Smithsonian* essay, Erdrich writes that the art deco movie theater, where she worked as a teenager, has been converted into a bar, and that the small café next door where she waitressed has been "stripped now of its ornate wooden booths, marble soda fountain, frosted mirrors and strange glass details into which were embedded the wings of blue morpho butterflies."[4] Certainly, changes have come, as they have in many small towns across America.

Wahpeton's population grew steadily from its early beginnings in the late 1860s to a peak population of just over 9,000 at the 1980 census. Then, the young people moved out in greater numbers and the old people passed on. Since then, the population has declined to around 7,400, but the town is not dead yet. The second largest employer used to be the 3M plant, but it spun off to Imation in 1997, closed in 2007, and was reinvented as Comdel—a company that makes medical devices, among other things. Other small manufacturing companies provide a few jobs for the community, but most of the businesses in town provide support for the agriculture of the region. Farmers here grow sugar beets and sunflowers and wheat, drink coffee at the little cafés in town when it is too wet to plant or it is winter, and the cows have already been fed. Erdrich hoed sugar beets at least for a while as a youngster among other jobs she held, both during summers and after school.

While her parents were both teachers in the school run by the Bureau of Indian Affairs in Wahpeton, their children did not attend school there. Erdrich says that she is not sure why that was; perhaps there was a school policy that prohibited it. She attended schools in Wahpeton, first Zimmerman, then Saint John's Catholic School, and eventually graduated from Wahpeton High School. Raised as a devout Catholic, Erdrich read the Old Testament from an early age and was enamored of the mystical, magical events she found within the pages, but she says that after she began school, she discovered that religion "was about rules." About her teachers, who were mostly nuns, she writes, "some were celestial, others were disturbed." Not a practitioner of any religion today, she says, ". . . I hate religious rules. They are usually about controlling women. . . . When it comes to God, I cherish doubt."[5] That honest statement is somewhat curious in a time when mainstream America views Indians as naturally spiritual, adhering to the traditional religious practice of their tribe of origin, and even American Indian scholars are wary of declaring themselves agnostic.

Family history and the inclinations of direct relatives do not necessarily insure that descendants will follow the same artistic paths. For instance, Mozart's children did not become composers, but the example of an artistic bent set by a parent would likely lead a child to appreciate whatever particular art form they observe. Erdrich has often mentioned that her grandfather, Patrick Gourneau, was a storyteller, and she has said that her father, too, was a talker. Orality has always been a part of American Indian tradition, but the urge to put those stories into written form was encouraged by Ralph Erdrich, who, it has been reported in many places, paid his young daughter a nickel for each story she wrote as a child. Few, if any, aspiring writers are paid for their stories from childhood, so early on, Erdrich would have learned that words have a monetary as well as an aesthetic value, and that writing for a living was a possibility.

Erdrich's childhood was as ordinary as that of any American child growing up in a Midwestern small town in the 1950s and 1960s. It was also extraordinary and unusual in that she had educator parents who actively encouraged her to write stories; she came from a mixed race heritage in a town where the overwhelming majority of the population was of mainstream European descent.

Like many other teenagers from small town America, she obviously wanted to see "the other side of the hill," because she applied for admission and was accepted to Dartmouth College in Hanover, New Hampshire. Erdrich says that her mother knew of Dartmouth and wrote off for information and admissions materials for her daughter. An Ivy League liberal arts institution, Dartmouth was founded prior to the American Revolution in 1769 by the Rev. Eleazar Wheelock, who had earlier established a school in Connecticut that was principally for the education of Native Americans. The charter for Dartmouth stated that the college was founded "for the education and instruction of Youth of the Indian Tribes in this Land . . . and also of English Youth and any others."[6]

Perhaps it was this history of attention to the education of American Indians that attracted Erdrich's mother, and Louise in turn, to this particular college or perhaps it was Dartmouth's newly established Native American Studies Program. Samson Occum, a Mohegan Indian and one of the first, if not the very first, American Indians to become educated and to write and publish was a protégé of Wheelock. Charles Eastman, a Dakota author and physician at Pine Ridge Agency in the late 1890s, was also a former Dartmouth student. If Erdrich had applied to attend one year earlier, she would have been denied admission, not because of her heritage or scholarship, but because she was a woman. Until 1972—the year Erdrich was accepted for admission—Dartmouth had been an all-male school. Even with the change of policy, for several years thereafter, men far outnumbered women enrolling at the school.

Erdrich's first year at Dartmouth was also the first year of the college's Native American Studies Program, where the man she would one day marry, Michael Dorris, was the director. In her keynote address to the graduating class of Dartmouth in 2009, Erdrich recounted her arrival at Dartmouth in the fall of 1972. She flew from her hometown to Boston where she changed to a small commuter plane for the final flight into Lebanon, New Hampshire. This commuter flight carried not only human passengers but also "livestock," as Erdrich puts it—baby chicks in cardboard crates behind a curtain, who peeped in terror every time the plane encountered some turbulence. Erdrich says she was terrified of being away from home, of going to college, of the plane flight, of changing planes at the busy Logan Airport in Boston, but the chicks had no awareness of being on a plane. Erdrich knew her situation all too well, and, she says, had some faith that the pilot knew how to land the plane. The chicks, which had no alternative but blind trust, helped to assuage her fears.

When the plane landed and classes began, she says she felt that everyone else knew so much more than she did. She spent long hours in the library catching up. She studied hard, but she also had to work outside the classroom and academic life. Contrary to what some people believe, she did not get a free ride. Her entire family sacrificed so that Louise, and later, two of her sisters, could attend Dartmouth. Part of that sacrifice meant that Louise had to work while attending classes. She worked first as a breakfast short order cook and later as a research assistant in the microfilm division of Baker Library. During her summers back in Wahpeton, she held jobs as a lifeguard at the city pool and as a flagman on a road construction crew, among others.

In college, she met American Indians from other tribes, including her Navajo roommate. She felt comfortable with Chippewas and Dakotas because she had grown up surrounded by members of both tribes, but it took her a while to get to know people from other tribes, and she frankly states that she did not understand the "non-Indians, the people who came from East Coast backgrounds." Further, "I hadn't left Wahpeton [before going to Dartmouth] so I only knew a particular Wahpeton mixture of people, all smashed and molded into a similar shape by small-town life."[7]

As educators, both her parents valued higher education, but they also must have missed their eldest daughter. Both wrote her letters. Erdrich says that her mother's letters were "newsy, full of recipes, fun, and practical advice," while her father's letters were "witty, anecdotal and intelligent."[8] She read with pleasure the following letter from her father:

Dear Daughter:

Your mother is making every sort of apple concoction known to man with the eleven tons of apples I harvested. She finds time for all of this because you left clothes behind. She only has to slightly alter those duds for your sister Lise who is rapidly becoming the best dressed eighth grader of all time as she inherits your ex wardrobe. Our house is steeped in apple juice and attracts half a million bees from all parts of the country. The insides of our compost cans have the fattest ants in all of entomological history. These critters have achieved their corpulent state as the result of the presence of the apple crap—peelings and such—which comes from the extra time Mom has—which is because Lise gets your duds. See how your going to college has upset the balance of nature?

Magnum est vectigal parsimonia. [Thrift is great revenue.]

Love, Dad[9]

His letter effectively illustrates Ralph Erdrich's command of language and vocabulary as well as his innate storytelling ability. No doubt, his children, including daughters Louise, Lise, and Heid, inherited that talent and were nurtured by his example.

Henry Hart, a poet and professor of English at the College of William and Mary in Williamsburg, Virginia, was a classmate of Erdrich's, both entering freshmen in 1972. Hart says that not everyone connected with Dartmouth was content with the decision to admit women to the college. He recalls that prior to enrolling at Dartmouth himself, he attended a dinner of alumni where an older alum pounded his fist on the restaurant table while declaring that, "Women will ruin the Dartmouth traditions,"—something that Hart found surprising. He had attended public schools in a small farming town in the Berkshire Hills of Connecticut where, he says, he was happy to be in the company of women. According to both Erdrich and Hart, the ratio of men to women for that first year of the coeducational change was 9–1. Hart recalls hearing the vulgar epithet of "quahog" hurled at female students.

Located near the Vermont border in Hanover, New Hampshire, Dartmouth's climate was not much different from that of Erdrich's hometown of Wahpeton, North Dakota. Both have long, cold winters with an abundance of snow and short summer growing seasons. Hanover in the early 1970s had a population not much larger than that of Wahpeton, excluding the student population of Dartmouth, which today numbers around 4,000. A major difference between the two small towns, though, was the terrain. Located in the upper Great Plains, Wahpeton is surrounded by rolling hills and rich farmland with a paucity of trees, while Hanover is surrounded by mountainous terrain well known for winter skiing opportunities. Dartmouth owned, and still owns, the Dartmouth Skiway.

The outdoor activities, particularly skiing, were one of the reasons that Hart was attracted to Dartmouth. There is no evidence that Erdrich ever skied, but Hart worked as an instructor for three winters at the Dartmouth Skiway, paying for much of his college bills with his earnings. Erdrich did know how to ice skate, and may have enjoyed that activity at Dartmouth as well as back home in Wahpeton.

Hart recalls seeing Karen, as she was then known, early in the fall semester of 1972, when she was walking across campus in front of the Hopkins Center, a kind of arts building known as the Hop. He asks rhetorically, "Why do you think certain people are uniquely beautiful and why are you immediately drawn to them?" He thought she was lovely, that she stuck out in a crowd, reminding him of his grandmother when his grandmother was young. Hart's grandmother was a Swede who grew up in a Christian mission, among other places in Mongolia and China during the early 20th century. He says that his grandmother and Karen Louise Erdrich both exhibited a pensive, reserved, tranquil personality.

Both Hart and Erdrich have each indicated that they were shy and reserved—something that Hart, at least, regrets because he did not get to know her better. They took at least some classes together and both attended a campus event known as Thursday Poets, a writing group that met in the poetry room of Sanborn House, where the English Department was located. Both studied with Professors Brenda Silver and Jay Parini, who admired Erdrich's growing prowess as a poet and mentored her. Hart says that he, too, greatly admired her writing, just as he admires everything she has done since their student days at Dartmouth.

At one point, the poet, George Starbuck, came to Dartmouth to read his own work and to discuss student work. At that time, Hart was fond of astronomy images in his poetry—something that Starbuck disliked. Starbuck was tired of moon imagery in poems, he said in a cutting criticism of Hart's work. However, Erdrich spoke out in favor of using moon imagery—something that endeared her even further for Hart—who felt that he had at least one poetic companion in the room. In turn, Hart was impressed by the poems Erdrich published in *Dart*, the student literary magazine. She had a more mature style, he felt, than any of the other poets on campus.

Erdrich indicates that her preparation for college life was incomplete, that she had some knowledge of Shakespeare because her father had purchased a record player and recordings of Shakespeare's tragedies for the family, but that her reading habits were indiscriminate. She says, "I worked hard to catch up with people. I didn't know any of the writers other Dartmouth freshmen had read."[10]

Her creative writing focus was poetry, and some of these early efforts appear in *Dart,* a literary magazine published at Dartmouth, which is now defunct. However, it was a student-produced publication sponsored by the college that flourished at the time. A paragraph on the opening page indicates that "We welcome poetry, fiction, and art work from all members of the Dartmouth community."[11] The faculty advisors were George M. Young, Jr. and Jay Parini.

The Spring 1975 issue of the magazine includes a short story attributed to Karen Erdrich, which was her given name. Later, she would drop the Karen in favor of Louise, her middle name. She says, "There were so many Karens when I was born. . . . I was happier when I was called Louise. I thought it had a good, lucky sort of writerliness to it."[12] The short story, entitled "Renny," is about a young girl who is stalked by a man in a stocking cap. The girl's parents run a bakery, about which the main character says,

> Mama was mad at me for being late. I was supposed to work right after school selling long johns and buns to people who had to buy things cheap. That was the only kind would buy in our bakery. The other bakery in town looked clean and hadn't a cracked front window. Their ways weren't no better than ours of baking. I knew. They were dirty in the back and just hid it better.[13]

While this is not the polished writing Erdrich would later produce, the above passage demonstrates the style of characterization that would become common in Erdrich's later writing. Here, the reader can see precursors of the kind of introspective commentary about other characters and situations that Erdrich uses for Nanapush and Pauline in *Tracks,* for instance. Here, too, is the poetic language that is typical of Erdrich's writing style. In "Renny," she wrote, "Somedays all it would take was the pure, thin tiddlywink of jesus." And,

> Stars turn on the pipes. Smokewater music. Dawn of bells and of windows. Ruby red for eyes, gold of gold and the black book and blue cloak and the pure tasteless Christ, blind inside me. It was almost as good as skating, walking down the aisle mouthing that floaty cracker.

Another section in this short story is more obviously poetry because the words are set off with wider margins from the main body of the story and the lines and spacing between words appear deliberately arranged to emphasize certain words. The poem is ambiguous, as much of poetry is, and here, it allows the reader to choose what actually happened to young Renny. Perhaps the stalker sexually molested her, but Erdrich uses a knife to represent a penis:

> . . . cold. black. hot.knife. and he
> had me with it and again he
> had me with it It
> had an eye and it looked all through me . . .[14]

However, she obviously was following the dictum given to every creative writing student—write what you know. Not to say that she knew exactly what it felt like to be stalked and raped or that she knew anyone who had that particular experience, but she knew what she felt as a young woman who might be concerned that such an event was possible, and to write from that perspective. She knew how it felt to be an adolescent girl who might sometimes chafe under adult authority. ("Mama was mad at me for being late.") She also knew about Catholicism since she was raised as a Catholic and attended Catholic schools. She artfully uses creative language to describe nuns and the priest at Mass:

> Crows, they look like crows at the altar. The bright man comes in with the golden cups. He sings, they flap about him, he sings for blood. The bells ring seven times. Three times the dark birds in the pews touch their claws to their breasts. Crows sing in the loft. . . .[15]

Quite possibly, Erdrich had sat often in the pew at mass, musing about the physical appearance of those attending with her. This same story also contains references to intensely cold winters, of walking to school in a dress (likely the dress code if her Catholic school forbade slacks), of "dumb farmers, clods, thinking they knew it all," which may sound hypercritical, but would not have been an unusual response by a teenager growing up in a small town, farming community.

It seems odd that Erdrich's first publication would be narrative fiction because she would focus on poetry for many years before publishing narrative in short stories and novels. In later issues of this student magazine, she published poems. The Fall 1975/Winter 1976 issues contain two overtly sexual poems—"Ode to High-School Sex" and "Night on Ward B." The first poem is a playful romp in the hay between "badboys" and "goodgirls." The last stanza reads,

> We will leap into hills with joined up tails,
> conspiring with spring. WE will catch the drunk plums
> on our coiled up tongues,
> as the continent of winter sinks!
> All tippling Ripple, we will tune our parts
> to the damned band of love, the golden
> dying of harvests.[16]

If Erdrich was a shy young woman in person, she was certainly not shy in print. The second poem reads like a horror story, as it describes a "simpleton," presumably an inmate of a mental institution who fantasizes about the nipples of a "servant-girl," who is apparently aware of his obsession, but refuses him her attentions. Part of the poem reads:

> Two pearls. A feast. But she refused
> somehow, and he was wroth,

and lost in longing—he cut them off
to fondle in his pocket till the day
they changed, grew hooks, began to bleed—
and then he fed them moths
till they grew wings
and flew, pink and shivering to her breasts again.

These poems appeared in the Fall 1975/Winter 1976 edition of *Dart* during Erdrich's senior year.

Poems published in the Spring 1976 edition of the magazine were quite different. Whether these were recent poems or something written earlier is unknown, but one of the poems, "The Hinterlands," seems to express a nostalgia for her home back on the North Dakota prairies, and may have been written earlier, when she first came to Dartmouth, or perhaps her time at Dartmouth had given her a new perspective and appreciation for her hometown. The second stanza reads:

When the sky pales and lengthens
and its cold ring of bone
vanishes behind a cloud,
I remember my home.[17]

The third stanza pays homage to the farmers that are the bedrock of the community, but the last two-line stanza seems to channel Yeats' famous poem, "The Second Coming," with that ominous ending—"And what rough beast, its hour come round at last/slouches towards Bethlehem to be born."[18] Erdrich's poem ends—"The fields, turning in sleep, cry softly/and something stops in the shadow of a barn." [19] It also evokes the early poems of Robert Bly. Another Erdrich poem, "Grace," is published on the facing page on the same issue of *Dart,* and it too seems nostalgic for Wahpeton, although the first line starts with the word "London." Erdrich had spent time as an international student at Oxford University in England during her enrollment at Dartmouth. The poem opens with lines about life in London, but goes on to a stanza that compares her mother's experience in North Dakota potato fields with the historic city landscape of London:

I dream of my mother picking potatoes
as a young girl on the reservation.
When her back hurt, she stood up
level with a cloud of grit
that whirled in the distance.
Probably she blew into her hands
as I do now—near a drafty window
from which I see
two towers of copper verdigris.

There is a sense of wonder at the differences between the two worlds Erdrich has experienced. However, where the previous poem ended ominously, this one has a humorous twist at the end, following the stanza written above:

Between them, the moon may rise, it depends
On popular demand.
If it does, I'll rub my eyes
& thank the Queen for planning the surprise.

Both Hart and Erdrich graduated from Dartmouth in 1976—the year this last edition of *Dart* was issued. Hart stayed on to work in and around Hanover for the next year, and Erdrich was still there, at least for a while, the summer after graduation. Hart recalls visiting her at her apartment on the outskirts of town. They talked about poetry, and he says it took him not a little effort to screw up his courage and show her some of his poems. One of them was a short lyric about a red eft, a newt that Hart would later revise and publish in his first book, *The Ghost Ship*.[20] Hart says, "I remember she had a book about seashells next to her when I visited her, and that I was thrilled to be with her one-on-one chatting about something we were both passionate about."[21]

The two would never meet again. Hart went on to a career as a poet, critical writer, and professor. Erdrich would return to her beloved Wahpeton, but within a few years, she would go back to Dartmouth.

NOTES

1. Lisa Halliday, Interview, "The Art of Fiction No. 208," *Paris Review* N195 (Winter 2010).
2. Flathead, Klamath, Menominee, and Potawatomi.
3. Louise Erdrich, "My Kind of Town," *Smithsonian* 37.5 (August 2006): 20–3.
4. Ibid.
5. Halliday, Interview, *Paris Review.*
6. Dartmouth College webpage, http://dartmouth.edu/home/about/history/html.
7. Halliday, Interview, *Paris Review.*
8. Sarah T. Williams, "The Three Graces: Louise, Lise and Heid Erdrich—Sisters First, Writers Second—Look Back on Their Parents' Hand in Fostering a Shared Love of Language," *Minneapolis Star Tribune*, Feb 3, 2008.
9. Ibid.
10. Ibid.
11. *Dart, the Dartmouth Literary Magazine* IX, No. 1 (Fall 1975/Winter 1976).
12. Halliday, Interview, *Paris Review.*
13. Karen Erdrich, "Renny," *Dart, the Magazine of the Arts* III, No. 2. (Spring 1975) (nonpaginated).
14. Ibid.
15. Ibid.
16. Karen Erdrich, "Ode to High-School Sex," *Dart, the Dartmouth Literary Magazine* IX, No. 1 (Fall 1975/Winter 1976).

17. Karen Erdrich, "The Hinterlands," *Dart, The Dartmouth Literary Magazine* IV, No. 2. (Spring 1976).

18. William Butler Yeats, "The Second Coming," in *Selected Poems and Two Plays of William Butler Yeats*, ed. M. L. Rosenthan (New York: Collier Books, 1962).

19. Erdrich, "The Hinterlands."

20. Henry W. Hart, *The Ghost Ship* (Crested Butte: Blue Moon Books, 1990).

21. Email communication with Henry W. Hart, June 24, 2011.

THREE

Grafting: Two Become Many

Louise Erdrich and Michael Dorris met when she was an undergraduate at Dartmouth and he was a professor of anthropology and the director of Dartmouth's new Native Studies Program. Erdrich enrolled in a seminar taught by Dorris, and they remained acquaintances—something that might not have happened at a larger institution with a student population of 30,000 or 40,000. Dartmouth's enrollment at that time was around 4,000. It was probably inevitable that the two would at least bump into each other on campus, but their relationship remained at the acquaintance level until after Erdrich graduated. For about a year (1977–1978), she worked as a visiting poet and teacher for the North Dakota Arts Council, and while she was working at this job, she began writing the manuscript that would become her first novel, *Love Medicine*. Continuing her education at Johns Hopkins University, she earned an MFA in 1979, publishing short stories and poetry at the same time. Dorris stayed at Dartmouth, earned tenure, continued as director of Dartmouth's Native Studies Program and adopted three American Indian children. Dorris and Erdrich continued sporadic contact, but did not meet again until Erdrich returned to Dartmouth in 1979 to give a reading that was entirely poetry—no fiction. Dorris attended the reading, and the two renewed their acquaintance and developed a friendship.

The renewed and deeper friendship not only brought them together, it also marked a turning point in both their careers. In a 1987 interview with Georgia Croft,[1] Dorris and Erdrich stated that in 1979, at the time of Erdrich's visit to Dartmouth, they had both given up on writing fiction, but after they renewed their friendship, they began collaborating on some short stories. Dorris then took a sabbatical year in New Zealand with his three adopted children, while Erdrich worked as communications director and editor of a Native American newspaper, *The Circle,* sponsored by the Boston Indian Council. Beginning publication in 1976, this was a newspaper format publication for native people, as their subtitle from the time suggested. Erdrich's duties at the time are unknown, but as both circulation and budget were small, she probably had multiple duties, ranging from general office work to writing some of the main stories.

While they were apart, Dorris and Erdrich exchanged personal letters and drafts of short stories. Although primarily interested in writing fiction, Dorris published some poetry in *The North Dakota Quarterly* and *Suntracks,* along with what he called some commercial short stories. Erdrich wrote her short story, "The Red Convertible," offering it to Dorris for criticism. By the time Dorris returned to Dartmouth from New Zealand, Erdrich had become a visiting fellow there; their relationship deepened, and the two were married on October 10, 1981.

This fall wedding between two people who were beautiful to look at, ambitious, and hard-working, who enjoyed working together, took place when the New Hampshire leaves were at their most gorgeous peak of color. Perhaps the colorfulness of the autumn leaves was a reflection of the colorful characters of both Erdrich and Dorris, with their unique collaborative writing habit that they had developed before their marriage, which continued afterwards. Indeed, in interview after interview over the next 14 years, both Dorris and Erdrich constantly emphasized their collaboration on writing projects that were eventually published under either Dorris's or Erdrich's name. Usually, the publication credit went to Erdrich rather than Dorris, which is not surprising. Erdrich likely had more time to create new works of writing since she was not employed in a demanding academic job as Dorris was and could more easily juggle her schedule to accommodate intensive writing. However, upon her marriage, Erdrich became an instant parent to Dorris's three adopted children.

Stepchildren, even if they are not living with the newly married couple, always require an adjustment for everyone concerned, and naturally, the more children there are involved, the more difficult the task. The oldest of seven children, Erdrich was certainly equipped to deal with multiple youngsters in the household, but Dorris' three were not ordinary children.

Reynauld Abel, Jeffrey Sava, and Madeline Hanna, all Native American children, suffered from Fetal Alcohol Syndrome (FAS) caused by their mothers' excessive consumption of alcohol during pregnancy. Alcohol crosses the placental barrier, disrupting brain cell development, which results in stunted or malformed cells. The symptoms of FAS vary, but can include malformed facial and other body structures and an array of behavioral and cognitive disabilities, including poor memory, attention deficits, impaired critical thinking, and impulsive behavior as well as the secondary symptoms of drug addiction and mental health disorders such as anxiety and depression. Dorris wrote about his and Erdrich's experiences in dealing with the problems of Abel (Reynauld), Sava (Jeffrey), and Madeline in *The Broken Cord* (1989). The book brought attention to the issues of FAS as well as to Dorris himself, winning the National Book Critics Circle Award for Best Nonfiction Book. It was named Outstanding Academic Book by *Choice* and won both the Christopher Award and the Heartland Prize. Awards and public attention were all well and good, but in the meantime, both Dorris and Erdrich had to manage the problems of their children on a day-to-day basis, and Erdrich probably more so than Dorris. He could escape into academia. Erdrich struggled to write as a stay-at-home mom. Perhaps writing was her escape, her solace, her comfort when the children's problems became overwhelming. Three daughters—Persia, Pallas, and Aza—would be born to the couple over the years of their marriage, bringing the total number of their children together to six. Certainly, financial success from their writing helped ease the burden somewhat by allowing them to hire help when they needed it. At the beginning, though, Erdrich and Dorris struggled like any couple on a single income living with and supporting three special needs children and their growing family with the addition of each of their three biological children.

The two continued to work on fiction, writing multiple drafts and trading them back and forth for intensive editing and criticism. Dorris said, "You get back this savaged draft, and then the arguments begin. . . . The objecting person always wins."[2] Early on, they collaborated on a series of romance novels under the pen name of Milou North—the first name a combination of Michael and Louise, and the North because they lived in the north. Romance novels are not considered respectable as literature because they are formulaic and often clichéd, but there is a thriving market for the genre. Erdrich and Dorris hoped it would make them a significant amount of money, but it did not. However, they learned the discipline of writing in a specific style for a targeted reading audience.

Erdrich did continue to write and publish poetry while perfecting her fiction writing. Then, in 1982, a relative informed her of a fiction writing contest, but only four days before the deadline. Holed up in her kitchen, she worked intensively and submitted her short story, "The World's Greatest Fisherman," to the Nelson Algren Fiction Contest—and won! That success broke the dam. That same year, Erdrich was awarded a National Endowment for the Arts Fellowship, and the following year, published both poetry and fiction. The poem, "Indian Boarding School," won a Pushcart prize and her short story, "Scales," won the National Magazine Award for Fiction and was included in *The Best American Short Stories, 1983*. PEN Syndication Fiction Project chose her short story, "The Immaculate Conception of Carson Du Pre," for publication. She still had not published a novel, although she had submitted both *Love Medicine* and another novel, *Tracks,* to publishers and agents. The rejection slips kept coming. In the early 1980s, then as now, almost no writer could get any book manuscript accepted for publication by sending their work directly to a publisher, who accepted work, particularly from first-time novelists, only through literary agencies. These agencies also hired a coterie of readers whose judgments on the quality, and especially the salability, of any work were final. Some of the major publishing houses received dozens, even hundreds, of manuscripts every month, so a cursory glance might be all that any reader could give to a particular writer's work. Often, it is not the quality of writing that gets a work accepted, but simply luck. Dorris realized this difficulty and responded by creating a literary agency of his own, even to having stationary printed. As a literary agent, he could then access publishers directly. With the advent of the internet almost 30 years later, such a ploy is unlikely to succeed because publishers can easily look up any purported literary agency online to determine whether or not they are legitimate. However, in those simpler times, the access that Dorris gained by representing himself as a literary agent and probably his persuasiveness in presenting her work got Erdrich's first novel, *Love Medicine,* accepted for publication.

While Erdrich uses multiple narrators for all three of the first novels she published, *Tracks* utilizes dual narrators. The storytellers in that novel alternate, with one narrator per chapter. *Love Medicine* and *The Beet Queen* utilize multiple narrators, and often, more than one within the same chapter, so that rather than hearing a solo performance, the reader "hears" a chorus. For instance, the opening chapter of *Love Medicine* begins with the death of June Kashpaw in a late spring blizzard, but segues into a kitchen table conversation among many of June's relatives who were important in her life. The few facts about June revealed here establish who she was, why she left, and why she is returning. This communal storytelling event posthumously establishes June as a member of the community within the web of memory while simultaneously telling the reader why June Kashpaw and her life were important. She cannot speak for herself, so others speak for her. The polyvocality of the plot here establishes the importance of communal rather than individual identity, and as these narrators speak of June, they necessarily reveal themselves and their own place within the web of family and cultural identity.

Erdrich draws not just upon her own experience and knowledge of Anishinaabe culture for this novel, but also upon her dual upbringing within both Anisinaabe spiritual practice and belief and the Catholic faith, and both are coded into this text. Hertha Wong has written about the elements of water and fishing in *Love Medicine* that she believes connect both Catholic Christian and Anishinaabe narratives.[3] For example, one origin story for the Anishinaabe states that the world was created on the back of a turtle, which is associated with water, and a later creation story begins with a world composed of nothing but water until a muskrat repeatedly dives down and brings up mud to create land masses. Such origin stories, known as earth diver creation myths, are not uncommon among many American Indian tribes. The geographic location of the Anishinaabe people around the Great Lakes of North America is sufficient to indicate that fishing would be an important source of food, and as any fisherman would say, patience and cleverness are important requirements for catching fish, and would therefore become integral values in Anishinaabe culture. In Catholic belief and practice, water is important, too. For example, water is a purification symbol in the rites of baptism, and fishing is a metaphor that Jesus uses when he recruits two fishermen as disciples, telling them that he will make them fishers of men.

Dennis Walsh expands upon Wong's analysis, but Walsh insists that the two worldviews wrestle for supremacy in *Love Medicine* when he wrote, "The Chippewa and Catholic codes are thus thrown into conflict though it becomes clear as the novel progresses that the Chippewa code has primacy."[4] In establishing identity for her characters, perhaps Erdrich was also working out her own identity, worldview, and spiritual belief, and it would seem that, for her as well as her characters, "the Chippewa code has supremacy."

The same year that *Love Medicine* was published—1984—Erdrich's first book of poems, *Jacklight*, was also published. Titles of poems and characters in these poems appear in later short stories and novels, as do water images. The second poem in the book is titled "Love Medicine" and contains these lines—"Still it is raining lightly," "she belongs more than I/to this night of rising water," "And later at the crest of the flood," "sheets of rain sweep up down/to the river held right against the bridge," and in the last stanza, "We see that now the moon is leavened and the water/as deep as it will go/ stops rising. Where we wait for the night to take us/ the rain ceases. *Sister, there is nothing/ I would not do.*"[5] [Italics in the original.] Another poem is titled "The Book of Water."[6] In addition to the water images, there are also references to other specific Anishinaabe images in such poems as "Windigo,"[7] which has a short definition of a *windigo* at the beginning. Catholic images are invoked as well, such as in the title of the poem, "New Vows."[8] While poetry is often image-driven or theme-driven, Erdrich's poetry is mostly character-driven. The reader meets people herein and not just the generic "I" or "you," "he" or "she," but individuals with names and histories, even legends. John Wayne is redefined through an American Indian perspective; the reader visits Francine's Room, meets Leonard who went each morning to the first confession, commits redeeming adulteries with all the women in town, and refuses to atone. Readers are also introduced to Step-and-a-Half Waleski, who will become a central figure in a future novel, *The Master Butcher's Singing Club*. Reading *Jacklight* is a retrospective of Erdrich's life to that point and a cryptic harbinger of her future work.

Both *Love Medicine* and *Jacklight* won multiple awards. Likely, she would have been proud of the novel's publication if it had been accepted immediately, but she was probably more so because it had been so difficult for her to break into the fiction genre. She had been publishing award-winning poems for many years, so a collection of her poetry probably seemed inevitable. Her short stories had also been very successful, but novel writing was an entirely different level of work.

A poem or a short story requires a quick concentrated burst of energy and concentration, then a period of reflection and revision, but creating a novel is a sustained effort over a longer period of time. It requires building a story with characters that hold the readers' interest through multiple pages, making certain that the words and actions of each character stay true to the persona the writer has created, building tension to a climax, and creating a satisfying ending. From the beginning and throughout the process, the novelist has to make choices—to write in first person or third person, to emphasize this character or that, to change a setting, and to make multiple other decisions that affect the overall tone and structure of the work. Further, the novelist must offer a sense of verisimilitude so that the story is believable and the reader will suspend disbelief. To achieve both those ends, the writer must ensure what filmmakers call continuity. If the novelist names a character Arthur on page one, then Arthur he must be throughout the entire novel. Mistakenly writing that character's name as Andrew in a different place not only confuses the reader, but undermines verisimilitude.

All of this is work intensive. In addition, the author needs someone willing to read and edit the work. Dorris provided this editing service for Erdrich, and she, for him. Most writers are not this fortunate. Those who are students in creative writing programs certainly get feedback on their work, but most of this comes from fellow students who are usually no better informed or talented at discerning good writing from bad than is the writer herself. Of course, workshops at the college level are led by teachers who must be published authors in order to get the job in the first place, and offer their advice, but being a good writer does not necessarily translate into being a good teacher, and simply getting writing—fiction or poetry—published does not necessarily mean that the work is good. It may get published because it fits a particular niche, as happens with some action films. These usually do not have a very well-constructed story or characters, but as long as they appeal to the mentality of 12-year-old boys with money to spend, they will be produced and distributed. That is simply good business strategy. Further, every writer has their own unique style, so the criticism provided by fellow students and the teacher, who may be and usually is, biased towards his or her own personal style, may in fact kill the style of a new writer, which can make the new writer's work unpublishable. Writers are usually not good critics of their own work, either. Some few are able to switch hats—to write creatively without thought for word choice or characterization or setting or continuity, and then to ignore the creativity that went into the work, while objectively editing their own work. Most people fit one category or the other. Of course, the element of luck enters into the equation as well.

The singer-songwriter Willie Nelson was once asked how much talent it takes to be successful, and he responded by saying that he did not know, but he did know that he would rather have a little luck than all the talent in the world. Erdrich certainly possesses great talent, but she was also lucky that Dorris willingly collaborated—or so it would seem—editing her work and promoting it as her agent. Alternatively, Dorris was lucky that Erdrich was willing to critically analyze and advise him in his own writing. Their marriage was seemingly a match made in heaven, as were their parallel careers.

The years passed and the publications and awards piled up. In 1985, the year after publication of *Love Medicine,* the novel won multiple publishing awards, but the most lucrative and prestigious award for Erdrich was the Guggenheim Fellowship (1985). These highly competitive mid-career fellowships fund a scholar, writer, scientist, or other professional for as long as a year. This would certainly have been a financial boon for Erdrich and Dorris as they struggled to provide for their growing family.

From that point on, Erdrich focused her writing energy on fiction, although she would continue to publish some poetry, as well as branching out into the children's book and creative non-fiction genres years later. *The Beet Queen,* her second novel, was published in 1986, and although it earned excellent reviews, was commercially successful, and was nominated for awards, it did not win any awards. The novel displays Erdrich's gift of describing human behavior through the actions and inner thoughts of characters, both White and Indian.

After being abandoned by their mother, the two main characters, brother and sister, Mary and Karl Adare arrive in the small town of Argus, North Dakota[9] on a freight train, intending to live with their Aunt Fritzie, but a sudden fright sends Karl scurrying back to the train, while Mary runs to her Aunt Fritzie's home. This early bifurcation in the paths of the siblings sets the theme for future events within the novel, which include the initial theme of abandonment, then separation, love, sexual obsession, and jealousy, and the aggression and self-destruction of which humans are capable.

The novel is replete with images and situations from Erdrich's past in Wahpeton, including the agricultural production of sugar beets. In creating a Beet Queen, she is following the practice of small towns that emphasize and honor whatever is unique about their town or region by naming a young woman as queen of that product or social practice. As Erdrich writes, "There was already a Snow Queen, a Pork Queen, and a Homecoming Queen. There would be one more queen and she would be queen of the beets!"[10] Here, Erdrich's talent for creating dialogue for characters that think and speak in thought-provoking ways are evident—"We are very much like the dead," Mary argues, "except that we have our senses."[11] The similes and metaphors that Erdrich writes to form the inner thoughts of characters are never clichéd, but always unique. For example, at one point, Dot, the Beet Queen from the title ruminates about Mary, "The Big Gal's is where Aunt Mary likes to shop. She's hard to fit, being built like a cement root cellar. . . . "[12] For all the obvious talent of the writing in this novel, the format is odd and the narrative seems disorganized.

In regard to the format or structure of the book, it is divided into chapters, but there are further divisions within some chapters, but not in all, and these divisions are sometimes indicators of a change of narrator, and sometimes are given imaginative titles, which makes the structure messy. That the novel was derived from 12 previously published short stories, most of which were published in 1986 just prior to the book publication, may be the origin of the structural problems. The book has a rushed feeling. Erdrich would manage reworking short stories for a longer narrative much better in her third novel, *Tracks.*

The following year—1987—saw publication of more short stories and more awards for the couple. That same year, Dorris joined the ranks of published novelists with his first, *A Yellow Raft in Blue Water,* which was nominated for multiple awards, but won none of them. The book, like Erdrich's novels is considered Native American literature, but it was very unusual in that most characters in this genre are either full-blood or mixed blood people; if they are mixed blood, the combination is inevitably White and Indian, as is true in N. Scott Momaday's Pulitzer Prize-winning novel, *House Made of Dawn,* Leslie Marmon Silko's *Ceremony,* and multiple other works by Native American writers. Dorris' novel featured a mixed blood protagonist who was of White and African American heritage. That was an unusual move, but it did not mean the book would achieve fame because of it. Perhaps Dorris did not mind that his work did not garner the critical acclaim and financial success that Erdrich's did, particularly since he contributed much to her work—something that she has repeatedly acknowledged and thanked him for. Perhaps there had always been difficult times in their marriage, and their eventual separation was inevitable when two such strong minded ambitious people are paired, but possibly, that slight to his published work began the breakdown in their relationship. The following year—1988—saw the publication of Erdrich's third novel, *Tracks,* which made it to that special place that every author dreams of—*The New York Times* Best Seller list.

She had worked on this book in various iterations for several years, beginning back when she was a student at Johns Hopkins, but it grew into a bloated manuscript that she could not seem to save, no matter how much editing she and Dorris did. She began cutting pieces from *Tracks* to use in other works, until, by the process of elimination, she had a much more workable manuscript that she and Dorris then reworked into a publishable manuscript. A short story derived from that novel, "Snares," was previously published in *Harper's* and then included in the *Best American Short Stories, 1988.*

Both *Tracks* and *Love Medicine* differ from other novels in that a chapter in a regular novel is not complete in itself, but may carry a thread of narrative from one chapter to the next in a more disjointed manner than in standard novel structure. One chapter taken at random from a novel is unlikely to be a satisfactory reading experience on its own. However, within the short story cycle type of novel, as most of Erdrich's are, each chapter can stand on its own with a beginning, a middle, and an end, but unlike a collection of short stories, the short story cycle has themes, settings, and characters in each story that contribute to a coherent whole. This style is common in Native American storytelling events, where one person may tell a story, which is followed by another storyteller with a related story, and then another and so on, like railroad coaches coupled together to make a train that begins in one place, adds cars along the way, and arrives at another place. Translating this oral tradition to written works would have seemed very natural for Erdrich. As George Bird Grinnell described:

> At formal gatherings a man might tell a story and when it was finished might say: "The story is ended. Can anyone tie another to it?" Another man might then relate one, ending with the same words, and so stories might be told all about the lodge.[13]

Two themes couple the story/chapters together in *Tracks*—the loss of land and concomitant loss of culture and community; and the influence of Christianity or Catholicism upon the Anishinaabe characters.

Land loss resulted from one of those historic moments, the Dawes Act, that Owens insists readers need to know in order to understand the American Indian novel. Also called the General Allotment Act or the Dawes Severalty Act of 1887, this law changed the definition and the reality of land ownership for American Indians. When the reservations were created, for each one, the entire block of land belonged to the tribe as a whole, so that no one person has a deed to a specific piece of land that could be bought or sold on the market. Neither the whole nor any part of reservation land could be sold or transferred to anyone else unless the entire tribe agreed and signed off on the deal. The concept of land ownership was alien to American Indians, who believed that land belonged to everyone, just as air and water did, and that people had the use of land, which might or might not be permanent. Any natural resources present upon the land—animals to hunt, plants to gather for food, trees for timber, water, fish within the water, and so on, were considered community property available to anyone, much like the concept of the commons in Europe and elsewhere up until the late 18th and early 19th centuries. Some influential people, Sen. Henry Dawes among them, believed that the main reason American Indians were not moving into the mainstream of American society and remained mired in poverty was because they had no pride of individual ownership of land, which was entirely a Euro-American concept that bore no relationship to American Indian worldviews. Dawes and his supporters introduced legislation that would break up the community-owned parcels of land on reservations and assign acreage to individual owners. Generally, each head of the family was allotted 160 acres of land, each single person over 18 years of age was assigned 80 acres, and minor children were to receive 40 acres each. Of course, before the land could be distributed, it had to be surveyed, and it is this process to which Erdrich refers in *Tracks*. The Dawes Act was signed into law in 1887, but reservations are vast tracts of territory widely scattered across the United States, which meant that it took years for the land to be surveyed. According to the dates that Erdrich assigned in her book, the surveying of the reservation there took place in the early 20th century. Other reservations in the upper Midwest were not surveyed and allotted for many more years. The Pine Ridge Reservation for the Oglala Lakota in South Dakota, for instance, was not surveyed and allotted until 1937, some 50 years after the Dawes Act was passed. The so-called Five Civilized Tribes of Oklahoma—Cherokee, Chickasaw, Choctaw, Creek, and Seminole—were exempt from the provisions of the Dawes Act until the Curtis Act of 1907 brought them under allotment as well. Angie Debo has effectively and thoroughly documented the severe adverse effects of these laws on American Indian tribes.[14]

Pauline Puyat, one of the two narrators in Tracks, claims that Fleur used the equivalent of black magic to kill or drive the surveyors mad, some of whom were tribal members. Fleur was of the traditionalist point of view, believing that it was wrong to divide up the communally-owned land into individually-owned tracts, but whether she actually put curses on the surveyors, as Pauline claimed, is open to interpretation. As Fleur said to Nanapush when he told her some of the rumors Pauline was spreading, "Uncle, the Puyat lies,"[15] which not only undermines the tales that Pauline tells to characters within the text, but is also a signal to the reader that Pauline is an unreliable narrator.

Another goal of the allotment act was to change American Indian culture from a communal social organization to individualism. It is unclear whether those advocating such change really believed that would help the economic situation of American Indians or whether that desire was borne out of fear of something they did not understand—fear that a socially communal group could unite under the guidance of charismatic tribal leaders to wreak mayhem against White citizens. The allotment act did exactly what its worst proponents hoped. Cracks appeared in the communal nature of American Indian societies as individuals, families, or small groups united to their own advantage over that of the community as a whole. Outside non-natives saw advantages in pitting tribal members against each other. Erdrich details this situation very well when she writes about the animosity between Nanapush, a traditionalist opposed to allotment, and the Morissey family, who took advantage of the new law to acquire their fellow tribal members' land. Even Margaret Kashpaw, common law wife of Nanapush, underhandedly pays the taxes on her own land at the expense of Nanapush losing his. Outsiders, too, participated in the land grab. The timber company in Tracks that acquired tribal lands through coercion, corruption, or theft is an example of the vultures that circled after the passage of the Dawes Act. A reader unfamiliar with the Dawes Act and the destruction it wreaked upon American Indian tribes may still understand the human emotions Erdrich writes of—the sexual attraction between Eli and Fleur, and between Nanapush and Margaret, for instance, but is unlikely to grasp the finer details that drive the plot themes of land loss and cultural disintegration.

The Christian missionary effort among the Indians, particularly Catholicism and the divisions it created, is a second theme within Tracks. Christianity is an exclusive religion; that is, its practitioners are expected to adhere exclusively to the Christian dogma that there is only one god and that is the God of the Christians inherent in the holy trinity of the father, the son, and the holy ghost. The central belief is that anyone who acknowledges other gods cannot also be Christian; however, American Indians have long been polytheistic, and most see no conflict between being Christian while simultaneously believing and participating in one or more traditional American Indian religious practices. For many American Indians, religion and spiritual practice are inclusive activities where it is common to attend a sweat lodge ceremony on Saturday and attend mass on Sunday. Such American Indians see no conflict. Erdrich demonstrates this common confluence of religious belief and practice within the character of Margaret Kashpaw in *Tracks*.

Margaret demonstrates her adherence to traditional practice when she performs the ceremony of setting the table for guests to bring people to her table who might offer information; yet, she insists upon attendance at mass, even though it means walking a considerable distance at night in the bitter winter cold. Pauline Puyat's heart's desire is to become a nun, even going so far as to inflict discomfort and pain upon her own body to prove her worthiness; yet, she still believes in Mishepeshu, the monster in the lake from Anishinaabe stories, and stages a challenge against him, although she seems to conflate the Anishinaabe Mishepeshu with the devil from Christian mythology. While Erdrich does not credit Christianity and Catholicism with the same level of destructive power as allotment, at least not in *Tracks*, she does portray Christianity as a divisive force contributing to the undermining of Anishinaabe social and cultural cohesion.

Pauline's eventual desire to become a nun is not so much about faith as it is about her denial of her Indian identity and her desire to become White. Early on in the novel, Pauline admits, "We were mixed bloods," and "I wanted to be like my mother, who showed her half-white. I wanted to be like my grandfather, pure Canadian."[16] She does not seem to realize that "Canadian" is not a race or ethnicity, but rather a national citizenship, and that Canadians may be any one of multiple races and ethnicities. At that time in her life, she did not want to become a nun, but only to learn the lace-making trade from the nuns. It is only when Eli rejects Pauline as a sexual partner, and Pauline turns to the aging Napoleon, gets pregnant by him, and bears his child that she decides to become a nun.

In the early 20th century, at least according to Erdrich's words in the novel, Indian women were not allowed to take final vows as nuns within certain orders of the Catholic Church. According to Pauline's narration, "For one day during supper Sister Anne announced that Superior had received word that our order would admit no Indian girls."[17] Here, Erdrich indicates that although Christians wanted to save Indian souls, they were not willing to completely admit Indians into Christian practices. The section also demonstrates the unreliability of Pauline as a narrator. Whereas, earlier Pauline had declared to the reader that she came from a mixed blood family, here she denies her Indian heritage in order to become a nun. The above quote continues, " . . . and I should go to her and reveal my true background. Which I did. And Superior said she was delighted that the hindrance was removed, since it was plain to see that I abided in His mystical body."[18] Obviously, Pauline lied about her heritage, but just as obviously, the Mother Superior accepted the lie. Living and working within this small community, the Superior would certainly have known Pauline's family history and known that Pauline was part-Indian in heritage. It can be argued that the Superior disagreed with Church rules about who could become a nun, and was therefore behaving in a humane way in knowingly circumventing the rule, but it can also be argued that this is an example of Christian Catholic hypocrisy towards the Indians that the Church supposedly served.

While Erdrich points out these hypocrisies, she does not tar all Catholic missionaries with the same brush. Father Damien, although somewhat of a bumbling character as the priest in the novel, seems of good heart and does practical things to help the people he is called to shepherd. For example, during one winter of starvation, when little game is to be found and other food supplies have run out, Father Damien "signs the paper for us" and brings them food. "In his pack he had a slab of bacon, a can of lard, a sack of flour, and a twist of baking powder."[19] When Nanapush, Fleur Pillager, and the Kashpaws are short of the money needed to pay the fees on their land or lose it, Father Damien adds the final quarter from his own pocket.

As well as being a masterpiece of storytelling, *Tracks* also effectively illustrates the devastating consequences of both allotment and Christianity upon American Indian communities. The complex characters, particularly Pauline Puyat and Fleur Pillager, are some of the most well drawn in American literature.

Erdrich's overwhelming success with *Love Medicine, Jacklight,* and *Tracks* might have broken the Erdrich–Dorris partnership and marriage at that point if Dorris had not published some minimally successful work on his own, but in that same year, Dorris' book about Fetal Alcohol Syndrome, *The Broken Cord,* was published, and in 1989, won the National Book Critics Circle Award. To match Erdrich's Guggenheim Fellowship from 1985, he also won his own prestigious award—A National Endowment for the Arts creative writing fellowship, probably based on his novel, *A Yellow Raft in Blue Water.* Now, the two of them had made enough money and had enough confidence in their financial future that Dorris could afford to reduce his academic work schedule and devote more time to his writing. He stepped down from his full-time professorship at Dartmouth to become an adjunct professor. Whether or not their marriage was stabilized by these events is not clear, but later interviews with Erdrich would indicate that they never had the ideal marriage that they encouraged the world to believe. The awards that Dorris's work won may simply have made him feel that his work was on an even keel with Erdrich's, temporarily calming the troubled waters of their relationship that was not obvious at the time, but became so later.

Erdrich, meantime, had gone back to her original writing genre of poetry and in the same year—1989—published another volume of poems, *Baptism of Desire.* Erdrich states in the notes for this book that it was written between the hours of 2:00 a.m. and 4:00 a.m., when she suffered insomnia brought on by pregnancy. The title of the collection comes from Catholic theological discussions and disagreements over whether a person baptized in ignorance of what they are undertaking is still saved from the damnation of hell.

Some of the poems in this collection, too, draw upon both Catholic Christian imagery and Native American, Anishinaabe myths and legends. The book contains five untitled sections, with the poems in the first section referencing Catholic ritual and mysticism while section four is made of up very short stories or narrative poems with Anishinaabe themes. The poems in Part Two are character poems that continue the narratives Erdrich established in "The Butcher's Wife" section of *Jacklight*. Part Three is a single five-part poem entitled "Hydra," and the concluding Part Five contains a dozen personal, reflective poems. *Jacklight* has a dynamic quality that invokes a sense of small town community as the poems move from one colorful character to another, from one major event in the life of a small town to another, but *Baptism of Desire* feels strained—a disparate collection of miscellany, with the exception of the section themed to Catholicism and the one referencing the Anishinaabe mythical character of Potchikoo, a trickster. The lack of overall coherency may be indicative of Erdrich's physical state of pregnancy, with all the changes that it brings. P. Jane Hafen chose to address in depth the Catholic-themed section and the Potchikoo section and how the poetry is rooted in Erdrich's dual upbringing, while ignoring the other three parts of the book. She wrote, "Much of Erdrich's poetry is a performance of beliefs derived from her variegated heritage, primarily Catholic and Chippewa." She continues, "Nevertheless, these poems also reveal a persona and communal voice. . . . Erdrich's poems manifest the paradox of individuation occurring within and being defined by communal and tribal relationships."[20] Hafen here succinctly states the difficulties of an American Indian person such as Erdrich, who must negotiate two sometimes conflicting sets of ideologies and worldviews, but Erdrich's poems do not seem to indicate conflict between Indian/Catholic worldviews, but rather, an objective acceptance of both. *Baptism of Desire* was not a great critical success and did not bring great financial rewards, but it was another respectable work added to Erdrich's growing list of publications.

Confidence in their financial future was justified when the two of them were awarded a joint contract to write a novel, *The Crown of Columbus,* for the advance sum of $1.5 million. The book was meant to pay homage to the quincentennial, the 500th anniversary of Columbus' discovery of America from the American Indian perspective. The beautiful, shy, young woman of Anishinaabe and German heritage from small town North Dakota and the tall, handsome young professor from Kentucky whose father had died when he was very young had "made it." They were the American Dream. The two were wined and dined, speeched and honored. Everyone wanted to shake their hands, and everyone wanted to interview them—from the most prestigious literary journals to small town newspapers. A selection of some of the interviews with them conducted from 1983 to 1992 was published as the book, *Conversations with Louise Erdrich and Michael Dorris.*[21] If they grew tired of being asked the same questions over and over, they never indicated it.

The May 1990 issue of *People Magazine* named Erdrich one of the 100 most beautiful people of the year. Each of the 100 people selected was given one page in the magazine with a short narrative and a photo. Erdrich was shown in three-quarter profile leaning against a birch tree with her arms crossed and an enigmatic smile. She wore a dark dress, a turquoise and silver bracelet, and a fedora with a blue feather inserted in the band. She is, indeed, beautiful, and probably felt very fulfilled at that moment, with her family of six growing children, if not always peaceful. The couple's three adopted children were always a source of chaos and conflict in the household, but she had a handsome and successful, if sometimes difficult husband, and a career that seemed to be on a never-ending upward trajectory. The career part of the dream for Erdrich has been mostly born out in the more than 20 years since that *People Magazine* article, but the family situation and her marriage to Dorris did not have such fortunate outcomes.

The reviews for *The Crown of Columbus* were tepid at best, damning with faint praise. A long review in *The Nation*, states:

> . . . there is a fair bit of entertainment—discounting some dreary chapters depicting the life of the dreary man who is a central character, and an interminable free-verse poem about Columbus recited by that same leaden man . . .[22]

This same review also points out historical inaccuracies of dates and events within the novel, continuing:

> It is a mistake not merely incidental but crucial, and for me fatal to the plot. Erdrich and Dorris, who write so convincingly elsewhere from their own experience, seem here to have been a little hasty in trying to exploit Columbus's.[23]

Although Erdrich's second novel, *Tracks,* had made it to the *New York Times* Best Seller list, that publication's review of *The Crown of Columbus* was not favorable. After a sketchy introduction that simply summarized parts of the plot, Michiko Karutani wrote that the book did not measure up to the works each of the authors had written individually. She is disappointed in what she terms as the lack of "strange, visionary magic," and complains that the while the narrative moves forward quickly, it is the same sort of thing that had already been offered in dozens of movies. However, at the end of the review, Karutani seems to have second thoughts about her heavy criticism of the book, and she wrote that *The Crown of Columbus* is still compelling entertainment.

A reviewer for the *Chicago Sun-Times* was a bit kinder. Reviewer Gretel Ehrlich wrote that the book is "historically provocative and outrageous," but that it is also fun. However, she goes on to criticize the plot structure and says that *The Crown of* Columbus cannot possibly be compared to great literary works such as *Anna Karenina* and *The Grapes of Wrath.*[24]

M. Annette Jaimes, a well-respected American Indian scholar, wrote a review that echoes the breathless, hyperbolic style of soap operas and the Milou North romance novels that Erdrich and Dorris had collaborated on years earlier—"Will Vivian and Roger find competitive happiness together? . . . Will their daughter out of wedlock, Violet, grow up to be somebody special?"[25] For Jaimes, the book is chock-full of every possible American Indian political and social issue, while including the social and psychological drama of American mainstream society as well. Her final words of the review are worth including in their totality here:

> At any rate, the bottom line of this paradoxical tale appears to be that Columbus' greatness is happenstance and trivialization of the conquest is acceptable, but nonetheless American Indians today have the chance to be prideful if not vindicated for their irredeemable loss. This book will no doubt be popular reading for the majority, but it is this reviewer's final assessment that the reputations of neither author will be enhanced by their team effort since in collaboration as literary artists they have chosen to engage in a pandering of their art.[26]

This less than laudatory reception faulted the plot, the characters, and the writing style, but not so much the already recognized writing skill of Erdrich and Dorris. In previous works by both authors, they had created characters that were not recognizably themselves. All authors, consciously or not, incorporate elements of their own personalities and lives in their characters. In *Crown*, the main characters are obvious reproductions and distortions of Erdrich and Dorris themselves. The heroine of the book is Vivian Twostar, a professor of Indian Studies at Dartmouth who is pregnant with her preppie boyfriend's child while simultaneously coping with a teenage son who is acting out. The boyfriend, given the historical name of Roger Williams, is a poet who wants to immortalize Columbus and thinks Vivian is beneath him, an amateur explorer and scholar.

Any reader who knows anything at all of the personal lives of Erdrich and Dorris would recognize the personalization of the characters. The authors chose to insert themselves directly into the narrative instead of creating entirely different characters that might have unrecognizable touches of their own personalities. The idea was a mistake, and one wonders exactly whose idea it was—Erdrich's or Dorris's—or if it was something mutually agreed upon. The novel seems uncomfortably formulaic, again recalling the Milou North romance novels on which they had collaborated years earlier. Certainly, they cannot be entirely blamed for a novel that, in the words of the reviewers, does not live up to works they wrote individually, which may be disingenuous to even suggest since they were open collaborators on works that were published under one or the other's name. However, they were awarded the contract for this novel based on a five-page proposal to the publisher, so the executives or editors at HarperCollins Publishing who agreed to the concept and approved the final manuscripts must also accept some blame for the result. Given the semi-celebrity status of Erdrich and Dorris, perhaps the editors thought that translating their celebrity into the plot of this novel along with their award-winning writing skills would create a book that could not help but make money. It did sell reasonably well, but the writing reputation of Dorris and Erdrich was somewhat tarnished.

The couple may have been privately upset by the book's less than stellar reception, but they shrugged it off in print. In an article for *The Chicago Sun-Times,* interviewer Wendy Smith wrote that "The authors take such comments [critical reviews of the book] philosophically."[27] Erdrich stated:

> We've had mixed, strong reactions to every book, because every book is different. We go with it. It's going to be the same book in ten years, so we live with the book rather than the reactions. [Bad reviews] happen to every writer.[28]

Dorris said, "I think that when you write a book you hope it's provocative, produces strong opinions and stirs conversation."[29]

They had reason to think philosophically and react mildly to the current criticism. Each had been through difficulties getting published in the first place, but had achieved remarkable success both individually and together in the preceding 10 years since their marriage. Further, as they indicated, they knew even the best-known, award-winning writers do not have a bestseller with every book they write. They already had the million-dollar plus advance in the bank. They could afford a bit of adversity, even mild rebuke. However, this setback was a harbinger of worse things to come.

On September 8, 1991, their eldest son, Abel, was stuck by a car. Hospitalized in serious condition, he died of his injuries on September 22. He was 23 years old. The newspaper accounts of what happened are sketchy, but they do report that the driver of the car was not charged, and that Abel had never learned to read traffic signals when crossing the street. Of course, the family was devastated, but possibly Dorris was more affected since he had adopted Abel as a three-year-old and raised him a single father until his marriage to Erdrich in 1981; Abel was the main subject of Dorris's award-winning book, *The Broken Cord.* The next two years would bring more literary awards for both Dorris and Erdrich, but also the denouement of their novel-like marriage.

NOTES

1. Georgia Croft, "Something Ventured," White River Junction, VT: *Valley News,* April 28, 1987, 1–2.

2. Ibid.

3. Hertha Wong, "Louise Erdrich's *Love Medicine:* Narrative Communities and the Short Story Sequence," in *American Short Story Sequences: Composite and Fictive Communities,* ed. J. Gerald Kennedy (Cambridge: University Press, 1995, 170–193).

4. Dennis Walsh, "Catholicism in Louise Erdrich's *Love Medicine* and *Tracks,*" *American Indian Culture and Research Journal* 25:2 (2001): 107–127.

5. Louise Erdrich, *Jacklight* (New York: Henry Holt and Co., 1984. Reprint, London: Abacus by Sphere Books Ltd., 1990), 7–8.

6. Ibid., 62.

7. Ibid., 82.

8. Ibid., 65.

9. Many writers have stated that Argus is a fictional town, but there is an Argusville, North Dakota, about 40 miles north of Wahpeton, which could have been the setting for this town that appears not only in *The Beet Queen,* but also in *Tracks.*

10. Louise Erdrich, *The Beet Queen* (New York: Henry Holt & Co., 1986), 304.

11. Ibid., 263.

12. Ibid., 333.

13. H. David Brumble III, *American Indian Autobiography* (Berkeley: University of California Press, 1988), 32.

14. See Angie Debo, *And Still the Waters Run: The Betrayal of the Five Civilized Tribes* (Princeton: Princeton University Press, 1940).

15. Louise Erdrich, *Tracks* (New York: HarperCollins Perennial, 2001), 38.

16. Ibid., 14.

17. Ibid., 138.

18. Ibid., 172.

19. Ibid., 191.

20. P. Jane Hafen, "Sacramental Language Ritual in the Poetry of Louise Erdrich," *Great Plains Quarterly* Paper 11–1, 1996.

21. Alan Chavkin and Nancy Fehl, *Conversations with Louise Erdrich and Michael Dorris* (Jackson: University Press of Mississippi, 1994).

22. Kirkpatrick Sale, Book Review, "The Crown of Columbus, Michael Dorris and Louise Erdrich," *The Nation,* Oct 21, 1991.

23. Ibid.

24. Gretel Ehrlich, Book Review, "A fun-filled, outrageous collaboration by Erdrich and Dorris," *Chicago Sun-Times,* May 5, 1991.

25. M. Annette Jaimes, "The Art of Pandering: A review of *the Crown of Columbus,*" *Wicazo Sa Review* 8:2 (Autumn 1992): 58–59.

26. Ibid., 59.

27. Wendy Smith, "A Novel Collaboration//Married Authors Compose Their First Written Duet," *Chicago Sun-Times,* May 12, 1991.

28. Ibid.

29. Wendy Smith, Interview.

FOUR

A Withered Branch

In spite of the tepid reception for *The Crown of Columbus* and the tragic death of their son, Abel, some good news did come to Dorris and Erdrich in the early 1990s. Dorris was appointed to the Board of Directors of Save the Children Foundation and received the Sarah Josepha Hale Literary Award in 1991. A year later, Erdrich received one award—from the Western Literature Association. The film version of *The Broken Cord* was released and won a multitude of awards. In addition, Dorris's novel *Morning Girl* won the Scott O'Dell Award for best historical fiction for young readers, and his essays on Zimbabwe won an award from the Center for Anthropology and Journalism as well as an Overseas Press Club citation.

The literary publications from both Dorris and Erdrich slowed in relationship to the sheer quantity of work they had published in previous years, however. While Erdrich must have been working on *The Bingo Palace,* their attention was elsewhere, dealing with the grief of Abel's death and the overwhelming family problems with their other two adopted children, particularly Sava, and Dorris's increasingly violent and erratic private behavior, which he effectively masked from public view.

The fourth of Erdrich's novels, *The Bingo Palace,* continues with the lives of characters, now older, that Erdrich introduced in earlier novels, while birthing further generations. Lipsha Morrissey, protagonist in this story, is the son of June Kashpaw, the dead woman at the center of *Love Medicine,* and the grandson of Lulu Lamartine, daughter of Fleur Pillager from *Tracks*. Lipsha has not lived up to an early promise but spent his life after basic education as a wanderer and ne'er to well, but has returned to his home. There, he visits grandmother Lulu, eventually seeking her advice in capturing the heart of a young woman, Shawnee Roy. His quest to slowly redeem himself is the heart of the story, but other characters and subplots intervene in the main plot line. Erdrich displays flashes of humor in the story such as the food fight at the Dairy Queen and Lipsha's vision quest from which he awakes, snuggled up to a talking skunk.

Back home with no marketable skills, Lipsha takes a job as caretaker at the Bingo Palace, a tribal gambling enterprise that is the forerunner of modern casinos operated by many American Indian tribes across the country. Lyman Lamartine, the father of Shawnee Roy's child and Lipsha's boss at the Bingo Palace, is a recognizable figure to most American Indians who grew up on a reservation in that Lyman epitomizes the typical wily politician who seeks power and influence, usually at the expense of the tribe as a whole. Erdrich would be familiar with this type since her grandfather was active in Turtle Mountain Chippewa politics, and undoubtedly told stories of similar real people. Indeed, Erdrich has likely met some of these tribal politicians herself.

The book is structured better than *The Beet Queen,* but is not as tightly written as *Tracks.* The reviews for *The Bingo Palace* were good, but that may have been because her other reviews were good—good news begets more good news, and critics were beginning to view Erdrich's works less as individual pieces but more as parts of a continuing, related saga. At least one review was slightly less than complimentary. *Publishers Weekly* stated, " . . . if the Bingo Palace is a capstone to the saga, as its interweaving of characters and half-remembered stories from previous volumes rather suggests, it disappoints." The concluding statement in the review suggests that the book is cluttered with too many stories, characters, and details that detract from what could have been a central theme.[1]

In 1993, while finishing *The Bingo Palace,* Erdrich was guest editor for *The Best American Short Stories, 1993.* Guest editor is a less intensive job than that of editor-in-chief of a group-produced volume. For the latter, the editor must usually first solicit contributions from qualified writers, then read and evaluate the submissions, choose the ones that most closely fit the overall theme of the work, copy edit in some cases (which means correcting spelling, grammar, syntax, and formatting), pester the writers to rewrite, when necessary, to complete rewrites, and finally to organize the submissions into a coherent whole. Guest editors usually have fewer duties. An editor-in-chief has already collected possible contributions, but still, the guest editor has to read through a mass of material, which is a time-consuming task, and decide which submissions are worthy of inclusion in the final work while remaining objective about writing styles that may be vastly different from the guest editor's own. While this work is rewarding in that it supports and encourages the work of other writers, at the same time, it subtracted from the time Erdrich had to create her own works. This may have been a respite for her, however, in that critical reading and editing required a different set of skills, which provided a break from her usual creative work. At some point in 1994, during what would be a tumultuous period for Erdrich, she penned an introduction to a book titled *The Falcon,* which was a reprint of a book first published in 1830, *The Narrative of John Tanner, The Falcon: His Captivity—His Thirty Years With the Indians.* Captivity narratives, published in the United States mostly in the early colonial period, were supposedly first person accounts of a White person's capture by a tribe of Indians, their subsequent trials and tribulations at the hands of their captors, and their eventual release. The most famous of these stories and the one that is most often the subject of scholarly articles about captivity narratives is the narrative of Mary Rowlandson, *The Sovereignty and Goodness of God,* first published in 1682. Rowlandson's story and other captivity narratives are polemics about the brutality of American Indians toward their captives and the goodness of God in saving the captive from the savage Indians. However, these stories give only the White captive's side of the story, without any details of the atrocities committed by Whites against the Indians that caused the retaliation.

John Tanner was captured by the Shawnee in Ohio and quickly sent on to the Ottawa Ojibwa. He was never ransomed and released, but grew up as an Ojibwa person who married and fathered children with Ojibwa wives. In his late fifties, he wrote his story, which detailed not only the circumstances of his capture, but of late-18th-century and early-19th-century daily life and customs of the Ojibwa people. The book was reissued in 1956, and again in 1994 with Erdrich's introduction,[2] wherein Erdrich writes that the 1956 edition was a part of her grandfather, Patrick Gourneau's library and that she had read it as a child.

Scholar Peter G. Beidler claims that Erdrich relied upon this historical background for much of her novels. He writes:

> One of the curious problems facing contemporary native American fiction writers is how they learn about their people's history, and one of the curious solutions to this problem is that these writers turn to non-Indian authors to fill gaps in their knowledge and understanding . . . [3]

Beidler's article goes on to cite historical references within Erdrich's novels as proof that she gained her knowledge from the John Tanner captivity narrative. While Erdrich may have borrowed and fictionalized some incidences from Tanner's story, it is quite a leap to assume that everything she knew and wrote about historical Ojibwa culture was gleaned from the Tanner story, without considering that Erdrich's grandfather may have valued the Tanner book not for gaining information that he did not know, but for reinforcing information he already knew. To assume that Indians can only learn about their own historical past by what White people have recorded about it is insulting. That may be true in some instances, but by no means, in all. The assumption may be because Indians transmitted information orally, and in mainstream society, if information is not written down, it is assumed to be lost. Erdrich never commented about the Biedler article. Perhaps she was unaware of it.

Dorris published two books during this time—*Rooms in the House of Stone,* which was a collection of essays, most of which had been previously published in periodicals. It was only 66 pages long. The other book, *Working Men,* at over 300 pages, was a much more ambitious book of short stories. This latter work garnered little attention, and seemed more of an afterthought. Another book, *Paper Trail,* a collection of essays previously published in such mainstream venues as *Family Circle Magazine,* was scheduled for publication in 1994, but would not be released until the following year. While the public persona of Dorris and Erdrich as enviable and glamorous literary superstars remained intact, their private world was crumbling.

Sava, the second adopted son, who had moved out some time earlier and was living in Denver, Colorado, began threatening Dorris and Erdrich, accusing them of abuse and demanding a payoff of $15,000. The couple, obviously afraid of what Sava might do, moved to an undisclosed location, and eventually pressed charges against him. In 1994, the couple traveled to Denver for the trial. One letter from Sava to Erdrich and Dorris read:

> Guess what? I am a bully. I pick on things weaker than I, I hurt them, and now I try to kill them . . . As long as I have friends that work in the Oklahoma police department, I'll always be able to find you. You can't hide.[4]

While Sava boasted in the note about connections to law enforcement, it is likely that this was an empty threat, but indicative of a disordered mind, probably symptomatic of his Fetal Alcohol Syndrome. His defense lawyer alleged that Dorris in particular had abused Sava, but his accusations included Erdrich as well. At trial, the entire jury did not accept that argument, but at least one juror must have thought the accusation plausible because they deadlocked on the verdict. A second trial resulted in an acquittal on one count and an 11–1 decision to acquit on the second count.

The decision indicates that while the jury may have thought Sava's behavior and threats were serious, they did not feel those threats rose to the level of criminal behavior. Whether or not Sava's condition as a child born with Fetal Alcohol Syndrome had an effect on the jury's decision is not known. It would seem that some jurors at least considered the possibility that Sava was truthful when he, through his attorneys, alleged physical abuse from Dorris and a complicity of silence from Erdrich. Perhaps this experience was the initiator of difficulties in the Dorris–Erdrich marriage, or perhaps it was only the catalyst for the breakup of a marriage that had been in trouble for many years.

Just four years earlier, the *Washington Post* had published an interview article with Dorris and Erdrich entitled, "Marriage for Better or Words: The Dorris-and-Erdrich Team, Creating Fiction without Friction."[5] The article reiterates what the couple had been telling interviewers from the beginning of their marriage and writing careers and what they would continue stating right up until the moment they separated—that they collaborated on every writing project, that neither let ego get in the way of producing good writing, that they used mutual criticism as an impetus to produce more and better literary works. Charles Trueheart, author of this particular interview wrote about Dorris's contribution to Erdrich's writing:

> "Michael," she [Erdrich] explains, is a "spiritual guide, a therapist, someone who allows you to go down to where you just exist and where you are in contact with those very powerful feelings that you had in your childhood." He organizes her work; he deploys a blue pencil on her manuscripts. He is, by her account, indispensable.[6]

In this particular interview, when asked what he might be writing or if he would be writing if he and Erdich had not met and married, Dorris replied that he did not think he would be writing fiction. He cites Erdrich's training as a creative writer and her experience as being superior to his amateur, untrained skills, but goes on to say that, "I came in basically as a suggester—very tangential—and in the course of time became more involved and more confident. But I don't think it ever would have happened without her."[7]

At that point in their marriage and careers (1988), there was no reason to doubt the sincerity of their mutual admiration. Only much later would Erdrich make statements indicating that she had resented Dorris's overwhelming and at times smothering influence.

Interviewer Trueheart asked a question at the end of the interview that was eerily prophetic and disturbing in light of the eventual Dorris–Erdrich legal troubles, marriage breakup, and Dorris's suicide. He asked if Erdrich would go on without Dorris, and she responded that she did not think she would, that she would not have the same sense of purpose. She implied that before she met and married Dorris, she believed that she would write no matter who else was in her life or what else what going on, but after her marriage and collaboration with Dorris, her feelings might have changed. No doubt Erdrich believed and felt deeply what she said in that interview, but seven years later in 1995 Erdrich separated from Dorris. Perhaps it was the strain of Abel's death and what must have felt like Sava's betrayal that brought them to the decision to part, at least temporarily. Perhaps, it was too much togetherness, contrary to their very public, frequent, and fervently stated appreciation for each other as collaborators, lovers, and parents, both in interviews and in the florid dedications each penned in the front pages of their published books.

The dedications in Erdrich's books are a love fest for Dorris. While her first book of poetry, *Jacklight* (1984), reads simply, "For my parents," in *The Beet Queen* (1986), she wrote—"To Michael, Complice in every word, essential as air." In *Tracks* (1988), her dedication page reads—"Michael, the story comes up different every time and has no ending but always begins with you." For the dedication in her second book of poetry, *Baptism of Desire* (1989), she wrote, "For Michael, The flame and the source." *Tales of Burning Love* (1996) has a cryptic dedication—"To Michael [heart]Q, [heart]J." Of course, the heart icon is an indicator of love, but the meaning of the "Q" and the "J" is unknown. The book was published in 1996, when Dorris and Erdrich were separated. Perhaps, the loving dedication was sincere, possibly mere habit, or maybe it was written to offer some solace to the man with whom she had spent so much time loving, working, and parenting, but could now no longer tolerate in her life.

Dorris was equally demonstrative in his own book dedications. In *A Yellow Raft in Blue Water* (1987), he wrote—"FOR LOUISE/ Companion through every page/ through every day/ Compeer." For *Paper Trail* (1994), he wrote—"For Louise: Absent by name/from most of these pages/only because/ you are so everywhere/within them."

The dedication that Erdrich wrote for her first non-fiction book is very different from all the previous ones. *The Blue Jay's Dance: A Memoir of Early Motherhood* was published in 1995, when the Dorris–Erdrich collaboration and marriage was unraveling. Her dedication here does not mention Dorris, but is instead a quote from Marianne Von Willemer (adapted by Goethe)— "You wakened this book in my mind, you gave it to me; for the words I spoke in delight and from a full heart/were echoed back from your sweet life." Of course, this quote could be understood as applying to Michael Dorris, but since the book is about pregnancy and childbearing, it would seem more likely that the quote applies to her children. Further, the dedication is not a few short, loving words to Michael Dorris, but rather a page of narrative that mentions their daughters, and in a second paragraph, mentions that Dorris wrote in their farmhouse in New Hampshire while Erdrich wrote in a little house across the road.[8] For a couple that trumpeted their collaborations to the point where they had said they sometimes could not tell who wrote what, they were obviously geographically separated in their work at this point. It could be argued that collaboration on a book about pregnancy written by the mother was not something in which her husband and the father of her children could physically participate with the same degree of feeling and understanding. One wonders, though, if Erdrich had deliberately chosen a topic that would make full participation by Dorris difficult. In fairness to her, it might be that the choice of topic was simply coincidental. Still, the subject of the book may have conveniently allowed her to achieve some separation between her work and Dorris's, and at the same time, to give her breathing room from the marriage.

Eventually the couple would move to a house in Minneapolis, where mutual friend and writer, Joy Harjo and others said that Erdrich decided she had to create a new identity, but she may have meant an identity separate from Dorris, so she moved out of the family residence in 1996, leaving the three girls with Dorris. Further, "She initially said she was going to move into a studio where she was going to write, but she left all her things. She left a nightgown hanging on a hook in the bedroom. Michael said he didn't have the heart to remove it. It was a symbol she was coming back."[9]

Their marriage—and collaboration—had lasted for 14 years, longer than many had anticipated. Michael Curtis, an editor at the *Atlantic Monthly,* never believed the collaboration would last long. "If it does," he said, "they will certainly have set a record for suppressed egos . . . Some couples work together and help each other, but none of them insist to such lengths and in such a firm way on their mutuality."[10] Another writer acquaintance of the couple said, "For any writer of fiction, it's impossible to believe any two people can write a book together. Something extreme had to come out of all this togetherness."[11]

In spite of Erdrich's assertion in 1988 that she would not be able to continue without Dorris, she did continue writing after their separation. *Tales of Burning Love,* published in 1996, probably had its beginnings while the couple was still together, but was likely finished after they had separated. Erdrich followed her established writing strategy by publishing four short stories that she later revised and expanded for the novel. Much like June Kashpaw in *Love Medicine,* Jack Mauser—the character at the heart of *Tales of Burning Love*—is dead at the beginning of the book, but brought back to life in memory by the stories his survivors tell of him—and of themselves. Two blizzards frame the story. Just before the first blizzard, a drunken Jack marries a young Ojibwa woman. Twenty-three years and four marriages later during a second blizzard at Mauser's funeral, the wives of Mauser, who are trapped together in a camper, tell stories of Jack and how each of them contributed to his downfall. This is a classic writer's technique for telling a story, one that Agatha Christie used in her mystery story, "Ten Little Indians," where the characters are trapped in an old mansion during a storm. However, Christie tells the story herself as the writer/narrator, while Erdrich steps back from the narrative and allows the story to be told by the multiple narrator characters of the wives. And, in Christie's story, the storytelling characters are not all one gender. In his review of the book, John Barrow quotes Erdrich:

> . . . there hadn't been a lot of books about women's closeness and women's bonds [when Erdrich began to write]. It was always there, this underground network. But women have begun to value their connections. It's often the case with men, too, I guess. But I wanted to write what I know.[12]

All of Erdrich's works were based on what she knew about growing up in a small upper Midwestern town, about being a woman of mixed heritage, of both American Indian and mainstream culture, and of human foibles. Since that is true of all her earlier work, it is not outside the bounds of possibility to assume that is true of this novel as well, which includes elements from all of her life to that point, including her relationship with Dorris. In this novel, she writes:

> Her marriage, though safe, kept her grounded. Her position as the wife of one of Fargo's leading citizens was both gratifying and constricting. . . . her every action was reported in the local news, her turn-of-the-century house was envied . . .

She was known for her original, even eccentric arrangements of flowers . . . her newspaper columns . . . she had become, in short, an admirable woman . . .[13]

Consciously or not, Erdrich wrote of her own most recent personal experiences, slightly disguised.

Erdrich's first book for children, *Grandmother's Pigeon*, was also published in 1996. This excursion into children's literature might be seen as a natural extension of the nonfiction *Blue Jay's Dance* about childbirth and early childhood parenting. The story of *Pigeon* is simple, as befitting a children's book, and is only 30 pages long, half of which are illustrations. In the story, the grandmother departs on a trip leaving behind three passenger pigeon eggs, mysteriously generated from a stuffed animal toy pigeon. The theme of environmentalism and colonialism is obvious. Passenger pigeons were once the most numerous species in North America but loss of habitat and overhunting made them extinct. Their nesting grounds and food sources were destroyed as European colonists arrived and moved inland, destroying wildlife habitat to establish farms and villages. Then they were hunted as cheap food for both poor American Indians and White settlers until the last one died in 1914. There are elements of the supernatural in this book, as well, notably when the grandmother leaves for Greenland on the back of a porpoise, a plot twist that has echoes of New Zealand Maori writer, Witi Ihimaera's book, *Whale Rider*. For *Grandmother's Pigeon*, Erdrich departed from her usual strategy of publishing pieces first as short stories, but the story does draw upon her personal experience. She stated:

I stopped writing poems and started writing children's books [the author says]. It's like a poem to me. It came like a poem all as a piece. And I worked on it line by line. It came from very much missing my grandmother, who was very eccentric.[14]

As well as being a challenge to write in a different genre, the book could also have been another way for Erdrich to express her independence from the collaboration with Dorris.

Separation and divorce is almost always a painful process for both partners. Maybe it is even more painful when the couple has had such a seemingly joyful and publicly successful union. Many couples experience bitter divorces with "he said/she said" accusations and protracted fights over money and child custody, but the Dorris–Erdrich breakup was about to descend into a horror that most couples never endure.

The emotional pain of the impending divorce worsened in 1996 when Erdrich and her daughters were driving back to Minneapolis that fall from a family gathering in Wahpeton, according to an article in the *Minneapolis Star Tribune* by Calvin Covert. One of the girls had recently seen a video in a school health class about good touch/bad touch, which prompted her to tell her mother that their father had engaged in inappropriate sexual contact with her, touching her in ways that made her uncomfortable. The other girls corroborated the first daughter's assertions.

Erdrich responded first by taking her children to Minnetonka psychotherapist James Fearing, and on December 8, Fearing reported the situation to child protective services, as he was required to do by law. Some may have wondered why Erdrich herself did not notify the police first, but the couple's celebrity status would have ensured a media frenzy, something she would have wanted to avoid to protect her children. She did take matters into her own hands, though, when she told Dorris that he had a problem with alcohol, and insisted that he enter Hazelden, an addiction treatment facility in Minnesota. The couple had shared custody of the children since their separation, but the abuse had been happening only during the last three months, the girls stated. Since the girls' statements are not quoted directly in the Covert article, it is unclear how specific their accusations are. Perhaps, in Erdrich's mind, there was the possibility that the girls had simply misinterpreted some innocent behavior on Dorris's part. She may also have felt that if he did cross the line, it was a result of his being so inebriated that he was not aware of what he was doing. Eventually, all four of the couple's daughters, ranging in age from 8 to 24, including adopted daughter Madeline who was not living with Dorris at that time, would accuse him of both sexual molestation and violent physical abuse. While the sexual abuse accusations from the couples' biological daughters were confined to only the previous three months, the physical abuse accusations went back years.

The girls stated to the authorities that Dorris had an explosive temper that erupted whenever they failed to meet his expectations. Examples of his violence included stabbing one daughter in the hand with a fork because, according to Dorris, she could not or did not hold her fork correctly. This same daughter stated that she needed medical attention after her father deliberately crushed her fingers in the kitchen door. Other incidents include kicking one daughter down the stairs, choking another, and striking them so viciously that they often had split lips, bruises, and bloodied noses.[15]

The litany of accusations was a continuation, perhaps affirmation, of what Jeffrey Sava had alleged in the court proceedings against his father back in 1994. In her own statement to the authorities investigating the case, from the article published by the *Minneapolis Star Tribune,* Erdrich:

> . . . confirmed that for years, she knew her husband "beat, hit, kicked, verbally and emotionally abused" their children. He once became so angry, she said, that he grabbed one of their daughters by the hair and ripped a clump from her scalp. She said such physical abuse occurred several times a month, yet she failed to report it until the final months of their 15-year marriage.[16]

This shocking and damning information destroyed the image of the perfect couple with the perfect family, as well as the image of the compassionate father who, prior to his marriage to Erdrich, has adopted three special needs children, wrote the definitive book on Fetal Alcohol Syndrome, and crusaded for children's rights as an active member of Save the Children Foundation.

Dorris's shining public persona did not deter the authorities from investigating the allegations. Katherine Quaintance of the Hennepin County District Attorney's office was appointed to handle the case along with two investigators. The day he learned of his daughter's accusations, Dorris called his friend, Douglas Foster, former editor of *Mother Jones* magazine and told him, "My life is over."[17] Despite his statement, Dorris tried to carry on. Released from Hazelden treatment center in January, he was soon on a book tour promoting his latest novel, *The Cloud Chamber*.[18] Like Erdrich's novels, this novel from Dorris was an intergenerational continuance of the characters he had created for *A Yellow Raft in Blue Water*. The first pages of the reprint edition of *The Cloud Chamber* cite no less than 32 glowing reviews from major publications and well-known writers such as Pam Houston, Anne Lamott, and Amy Tan. The last words of the dedication read—" . . . to Louise, my love and gratitude for all of it."[19]

In March of 1997, investigators traveled to Colorado to interview Sava and Madeline about their father's possible sexual and physical abuse. At first, Madeline denied being victimized by her father, but eventually she said she had been abused, and Sava confirmed her statements.[20] After learning of this event, on the night of March 28, 1997, Dorris went back to the house in New Hampshire where he and Erdrich and the children had lived for so many years. Then he went to the cottage across the road from the main house—the cottage where Erdrich had worked separately from Dorris when their marriage and writing collaboration had begun to come apart—and swallowed pills and alcohol. He answered the phone from there when his friend, Doug Foster, called. From the conversation, Foster became aware that something was terribly wrong. He called the state police, who transported Dorris to the hospital and from there to Brattleboro Retreat in Vermont. Apparently, Dorris was angry with his friend for interfering.[21]

Erdrich was notified, but as far as anyone knows, she did not contact Dorris. In an interview for the *Seattle Intelligencer,* Erdrich stated, "I knew that Michael was suicidal from the second year of our marriage, . . . he talked about it often."[22] After 13 years of hearing Dorris threaten suicide, of trying to be kind and understanding and comforting, any human, no matter how much they loved the suicidal spouse, is likely to become wearied by the exercise. The common statement is that suicide is a cry for help, and that may be true in most cases, but how many times can the cry be addressed before those trying to help begin to wonder if the suicide threats are more of an attention-getting device rather than a sincere desire to get past psychic or physical pain?

From 1972–1977, NBC television ran *Sanford and Son,* a half hour sitcom starring Redd Foxx as junkyard owner, Fred Sanford, and Demond Wilson as Fred's son, Lamont. The irascible character of Fred constantly got himself into trouble through foolish mistakes or deliberate lies and misbehavior. When Fred's misdeeds were discovered by Lamont, Fred's usual reaction was to fake a heart attack to get sympathy. While it is doubtful that Dorris would behave so obviously as Fred Sanford, perhaps he engaged in more subtle but similar behavior. A reasonable person could have believed that if Dorris had really wanted to die, he would not have answered the phone call from Foster. The next time, however, Dorris was serious.

Dartmouth had planned a celebration on April 11 for the 25th anniversary of the founding of their Native American Studies Program and had asked Dorris to speak at the event since he was the first director of that program. Dorris got a pass from Brattleboro and traveled to a nearby hotel, The Brick Tower Inn. He must have been very determined that there could be no interference this time because he parked his car in the parking lot of a different motel across the street and registered at the Brick Tower Inn under the name of George Fonta. There he swallowed a massive dose of sleeping pills along with substantial quantities of vodka and covered his head with a plastic bag. His body was discovered the next day, the same day he was to have been charged by the Hennepin County (Minnesota) Attorney's Office with criminal sexual child abuse. Dorris's death ended the investigation, but did not silence the matter. From then on, his entire life and work as well as that of Erdrich would be put under the microscope. In death, he managed to escape public scrutiny over whether or not he was a physically and sexually abusive father. His suicide, however, only added another layer of scandal that Erdrich and her children had to endure.

Humans have an insatiable desire to know why things happen, especially so if the event that happened is of a shocking or prurient nature, and not only to know why, but to find someone to blame. Erdrich, dealing with the trauma of her marriage breakup first, then her children's accusations against their father, now had to deal with Dorris's suicide, and the inevitable horde of reporters and others who wanted to dig around not only in her life, but in her psyche as well. There were those who judged her complicit in Dorris's physical abuse of their children, if not in Dorris's sexual abuse, which might have been either confirmed or dismissed had he lived and the case came to trial.

Calvin Covert, in the article that he wrote months after Dorris's suicide, did not directly go after Erdrich as a contributing factor in the children's abuse, but his bald statements were damning in such words as—"She [Erdrich] never filed a police report about the child beatings she said she had witnessed."[23] Covert's article was published four months after Dorris's suicide, proof that the story was still of interest to the reading public.

Erdrich had wisely tried to anticipate and dampen the firestorm that was to come with the interview she granted to the *Seattle Post-Intelligencer* on April 19, just eight days after Dorris's suicide. The newspaper interviewer wrote, "Now, Erdrich said, she wanted to talk about their lives and the circumstances surrounding his death—to correct some misconceptions" that "seem to be floating around in the media" and to help shift the emphasis from the "grotesque details" of Dorris' death and the "morbid fascination" with the most intimate details of their private troubles."[24] Undoubtedly, Erdrich's first consideration was to protect her children from painful gossip and innuendo by trying to offer factual information. She tried to get out ahead of the story, as politicians say when scandals break.

Of Dorris's friends and acquaintances, most did not believe the sexual abuse and other physical abuse allegations. For example, according to the *Washington Post* article of April 16, "Charles Rembar, a New York lawyer who represented the couple in literary matters said that 'on the basis of a long and close relationship with Michael Dorris, I regard the charges as utterly implausible.'" In the same article, writer Robb Forman Dew stated, "He has always been an advocate for children. Every instinct I have tells me this is as unlikely as anything I've ever heard."[25]

Friends and acquaintances were equally disbelieving about Erdrich's statements of Dorris's long-standing suicidal thoughts. The *Seattle Post-Intelligencer* article stated—"Indeed, close friends of Dorris have said in recent interviews that they found it difficult to believe that the generous, brilliant and gregarious man they knew was secretly tormented by depression and thoughts of suicide."[26] Oddly enough, even Douglas Foster, the friend who had rescued Dorris from the first attempted suicide on March 28, said, "He may have had his dark moments, but to say that he was fixated on suicide, I didn't see it."

Erdrich's statements contradict those of Dorris's friends. She said that the friends and colleagues who were disbelieving of Dorris's mental state did not know of his "private suffering" because Dorris kept those feelings hidden. In her writer's language of metaphor and simile, Erdrich stated that the picture Dorris presented to the world was like the third floor of building with a "very deep basement." While his friends may have been oblivious to the real Dorris, Erdrich said that she knew of his personal anguish.[27]

The most painful press story of all may have been Eric Konigsberg's June 16 article in *The New Yorker*. Before it came out in print, Konigsberg tracked Erdrich down at her home in Minneapolis to tell her what he had written and maybe to get her response to it. He came to her house unannounced, an act that must have made her feel trapped and besieged. From a journalistic standpoint, the Konigsberg article is well-written and includes some documented facts, but it also implies much—that Dorris may have engaged in homosexual liaisons, something that no other article had done. Erdrich may have felt it was better to let such allegations lie rather than to refute them in print and so keep the information in circulation. If so, she was right. No other publication picked up on the Konigsberg speculations about Dorris's sexual proclivities.

The public enjoys creating celebrities and heroes, placing them on an impossibly high pedestal and worshipping them, but it takes just as great a delight in pulling down those same celebrities and heroes. Perhaps there is some perverse pleasure to be had in discovering that the perfect couple is beset by some of the same problems or even worse ones than ordinary people. To paraphrase Charles Dickens, the marriage and literary collaboration of Michael Dorris and Louise Erdrich was the best of times, and it was the worst of times.

NOTES

1. Review of *The Bingo Palace, Publishers Weekly*, January 31, 1994.
2. John Tanner, *John Tanner, The Falcon* (New York: Perennial, 1994).
3. Peter G. Beidler, "The Facts of Fictional Magic: John Tanner as a Source for Louise Erdrich's *Tracks* and *The Birchbark House*," *American Indian Culture and Research Journal* 24:4 (2000): 37–54.
4. David Streitfeld, "Writer Was Suspected of Child Abuse: Probe Ends with Michael Dorris Suicide," *The Washington Post,* Apr 16, 1997.
5. Charles Trueheart, "Marriage for Better or Words," *The Washington Post,* October 19, 1988.
6. Ibid.
7. Ibid.
8. Louise Erdrich, *The Blue Jay's Dance: A Memoir of Early Motherhood* (New York: HarperCollins Publishing, 1995), vii–viii.
9. Streitfeld, *The Washington Post.*
10. Ibid.
11. Susan Shreve, quoted in Streitfeld article, *The Washington Post.*
12. John Barrow, "All the Right Connections//Louise Erdrich Adds 'Burning Love' to Other Related Tales," Chicago Sun Times, May 26, 1996.
13. Louise Erdrich, *Tales of Burning Love* (New York: First Harper Perennial, 1997), 220.
14. John Barrow, Interview and Review.
15. Specific information included here comes from Calvin Covert's article, "The Anguished Life of Michael Dorris," published in the *Minneapolis Star Tribune* on August 2, 1997, almost four months after Dorris's death. While the information is graphic, Covert states that the information contained in the story was obtained from "interviews with the couples friends, neighbors, and professional peers; court, police, and child-protection records in the Twin Cities, New Hampshire, and Colorado; two lawsuits filed against Dorris's estate and Erdrich by their adopted daughter, Madeline, and Dorris's memoirs." Erdrich did not sue the paper for false statements, which does not necessarily mean the information was correct, only that Erdrich did not choose to contest the content.
16. Ibid.
17. Covert article in the *Minneapolis Star Tribune.*
18. Michael Dorris, *The Cloud Chamber* (San Diego: Paw Prints Imprint of Baker and Taylor Publishing, 2008, Reprint).
19. Ibid., 9.
20. Eric Konigsberg, "The Last Page," *The New Yorker,* June 16, 1997, 31–37, 70.
21. Ibid.
22. Staff writer, "Wife Claims Dorris was Suicidal for Years, Only She Knew of His Tormented Secret Life," *Seattle Post-Intelligencer,* April 19, 1997.
23. Covert article in *The Minneapolis Star Tribune.*
24. Article in *Seattle Post-Intelligencer,* April 19, 1997
25. Streitfeld, *The Washington Post.*
26. *Seattle Post-Intelligencer,* April 19, 1997.
27. Ibid.

FIVE

New Shoots from Old Roots

After Dorris's death, Erdrich moved back into the house in Minneapolis where Dorris had lived with their three daughters. She went on with her writing and raising her daughters, even reconciled with Madeline, the adopted daughter who had accused Dorris of physical and sexual abuse. Whether or not those allegations from Madeline and Sava and from the couple's three biological daughters were true or not is unknowable. Erdrich herself testified to the validity of the physical violence, but the sexual abuse is questionable. It is possible that their biological daughters mistook innocent acts of affection or drunken fumblings from Dorris for more than what they were, and it must be remembered that Madeline, who claimed sexual abuse as well, and Sava, who supported Madeline's statement, were both Fetal Alcohol Syndrome children. These children naturally have difficulty in distinguishing reality from fiction.

Pressed by the Minneapolis prosecutor Katherine Quaintance and her investigators, Madeline and Sava were likely to have said what they believed these people in positions of authority expected to hear. Such situations are not uncommon. There are numerous instances of innocent people with mental disabilities testifying that they committed or were witnesses to crimes they could not possibly have committed or witnessed.

Erdrich sought comfort, security, and love from her parents, Ralph and Rita Erdrich, from her brothers and sisters and their families, and from the community where she grew up. She wrote:

> My brothers are loyal and kind fellows, and they have seen me through tough times. When my husband died in 1997 they took off work to come and stay with me, to answer the telephone and guard my children. They also made sure I didn't stay in bed all day, chew the woodwork, or just sit in the corner and drool. They helped the household keep on functioning. They kept my world partly normal. They are tall and sturdy and they make me feel safe.[1]

Her work and her children were in Minneapolis where she lived, but there were frequent trips home to Wahpeton and to Turtle Mountain, where she was not the famous writer at the center of a scandal, but just Louise—daughter, sibling, and friend.

Back in 1988, when Louise Erdrich told an interviewer that she would not go on [writing] without Michael Dorris, she was no doubt sincere, but by 1996, when she separated from him and filed for divorce, she had changed her mind or maybe, came to know her own mind better. After his suicide in 1997, she had no choice but to go on without him. They had claimed that they wrote in collaboration, that at times it was hard to tell who wrote what in any published work, so after the separation and Dorris's subsequent suicide, readers at least, if not publishers, were curious to discover if the writing Erdrich did on her own would be of the same quality, quantity, and style as the work she published with Dorris as editor and collaborator.

The Antelope Wife, her sixth novel (not counting *The Crown of Columbus,* written as a stated collaboration with Dorris), was published in 1998. The Acknowledgements page of the novel begins with, "As always, my family is first in my thanks," and continues with expressions of gratitude to specific family members, indicating that she had, indeed, relied upon them for comfort and support during the year of her separation from Dorris and, following his death, the painful public revelations—true or false—about their life together and apart. The comments about beadworking in this section mirror the beadworking motif that runs throughout *The Antelope Wife.* Erdrich's real life off the page blurred into the writing on the page, as was always true.

The dedications in almost all her other books were to Dorris, but the one for *The Antelope Wife* reads:

TO MY CHILDREN,
   PERSIA, AZA
   PALLAS, BIRDIE
   AND SAVA

She included all the living children, even Sava, though there is no evidence that they had reconciled their differences at that time. (Note that Birdie was the family nickname for Madeline.) Another page—more of a disclaimer than a dedication—is inserted at the front of the book. It reads—*This book was written before the death of my husband. He is remembered with love by all of his family.* Here, Erdrich speaks for herself and for all the children—even the daughters who had accused Dorris of child abuse. If Dorris had lived, been prosecuted, and found guilty, this page would almost certainly not be included, but Erdrich has stated elsewhere that she believes the dead should be left in peace. That may be the reason for this disclaimer in *The Antelope Wife,* but it is also likely that she felt she had to say *something* to forestall possible speculation since so many of the themes and events in the novel seem to bear on her own personal life.

The files of the investigation had been sealed after Dorris's death, a common practice, but also something that Erdrich had urged. Further, in the *Seattle Post-Intelligencer* article from just days after Dorris's suicide, Erdrich said specifically that the strange and difficult circumstances surrounding the family accusations against Dorris and his subsequent suicide was a private, family matter, and that generally, she ascribed to the idea that public gossip and speculation about any person after they had died was unconscionable.[2]

Another novel with mostly American Indian characters, *The Antelope Wife* is written in Erdrich's usual style—flowing poetic or descriptive sentences followed by short cryptic sentences, or even incomplete sentences, such as the following:

> In chaos of groaning horses, dogs screaming, rifle and pistol reports, and the smoke or errant cooking fires, Scranton Roy was most disturbed not by the death yells of old men and the few warriors shocked naked from their robes, but by the feral quiet of the children. And the sudden contempt he felt for them all. Unexpected, the frigid hate.[3]

This novel proved that Erdrich's solitary writing was as good as her collaboration writing with Dorris and not just in style and plot. In her previous novels, there is a great deal of humor, and she continues to use humor to humanize her characters, to forward plot structures, and to lighten dark moments. Much of the humor she included in previous novels arises out of cultural perspectives from her own Anishinaabe heritage. For example, the character of Nanapush in *Tracks* is a classical trickster figure common in Native American oral tradition and mythology.

In American Indian cultures, trickster figures are characters that usually have an animal counterpart, which varies depending upon the tribe of origin. Among tribes in the Northeast, Great Rabbit is the common figure, while Southwestern tribes reference Coyote in their stories. Iktomi, the Spider, is the trickster figure in stories from the Great Plains tribes, but in the Northwestern United States and Canada, the Raven is the animal/human trickster figure. Greediness for food, drink, and money; arrogance and selfishness; sexual promiscuity; bawdy humor; and gender switching are all characteristic of trickster figures. Usually the trickster attempts to con someone out of something of value—typically, food or sexual favors. Because the trickster is also inept, he inevitable bungles his own con, and in so doing creates something of value, even if it is only the lesson that greediness does not pay. The result of his behavior is serendipitous. From the seeds of disaster, something wonderful grows. While scholars recognize the trickster figure in American Indian stories, less often do they acknowledge that such figures exist in the literature and stories of other cultures. The gnomes of Scandinavian cultures are one example, as are the fairies and elves of Ireland.

Nanapush does not appear to have a directly recognizable animal counterpart, but his trickster qualities are evident throughout *Tracks*. He utters bawdy, sexually explicit comments to Pauline, the young Anishinaabe woman who aspires to be a nun, and to his former trapping partner's wife, Margaret, who later becomes Nanapush's lover. He has no compunctions about making anatomical jokes with the priest at the local church. Nanapush complains about the hard seats in the church, and Father Damien replies, "You must think of their unyielding surfaces as helpful," he offered. "God sometimes enters the soul through the humblest parts of our anatomies, if they are sensitized to suffering." Nanapush makes a typical trickster response, "A god who enters through the rear door," I countered, "is no better than a thief."[4]

As in her earlier works, the humor Erdrich utilizes in *The Antelope Wife* is often situational, such as that embodied in the character of Cecille, the ditsy relative of Rozina's lover and later husband, Frank. Cecille is a good person, a hardworking martial arts instructor, but she also embroiders the truth, creating fantastic, often funny stories about everyday events in her life. One such incidence is when the women are in the kitchen preparing for the marriage of Rozina and Frank. Cecille begins one of her long-winded stories, but no one listens to her, with tragic results because when Cecille informs the group that Rozina's ex-husband, Richard, is going to show up at the event, no one believes her. Of course, Richard does show up, creating a violent and embarrassing, though humorous, scene.

Toward the end of the book, Erdrich includes another incident of situational humor at Rozina and Frank's first wedding anniversary. Both characters want to please the other, so Frank lets Rozina believe it will be a private celebration with just the two of them, even though he knows Rozina would prefer to have family and friends present. Frank plans a surprise party, where Rozina shows up almost completely naked, believing the two will be alone. She is surprised and embarrassed when she discovers other people are present. Author Lorena Stookey, in her book about Erdrich's work, discusses this incident as a reference to O. Henry's classical story, "The Gift of the Magi," where two lovers want to please each other with a perfect Christmas gift, but, through a turn of fate, each one's gift is made useless by the other's gift.[5] Stookey cites this situation in *The Antelope Wife* as a "comic retelling" of the O. Henry story,[6] and also notes humor as a grounding theme in Erdrich's works.[7]

One of the funniest sections in *The Antelope Wife* concerns the reservation dog, Almost Soup, who is given a human voice with human emotions, especially fear of death and the urge to survive. For readers who are not American Indian or did not grow up on a reservation, much in this section may be glossed over or misunderstood as akin to children's stories where animals talk and have feelings. Dogs are ubiquitous on reservations; they are family pets, feral animals, and strays. Indians are aware, of course, that neutering and spaying are humane practices that cut down on the number of unwanted animals doomed to suffer and die, but poverty is as rampant on reservations as stray animals. When it is a choice between food or a vet bill, people have to choose food.

The role of dogs is usual in ceremonial practice for tribes of the Great Plains, where a dog—usually a white puppy—is ceremonially sacrificed and boiled. The resulting soup with small bits of the flesh is consumed by people as a healing rite rather than a secular meal. The character of Almost Soup is very aware of this practice and is determined not to become the sacrificial dog. This section of the book, the beginning of Part Two, is written in second person. The dog addresses the reader as "you," as if the reader is a dog to whom Almost Soup is giving advice after recounting his own family background and his story of surviving the soup pot. His advice includes such items as:

> Eat anything you can at any time. Fast. Bolt it down. Stay cute, but stay elusive. Don't let them think twice when they've got the hatchet out . . . Avoid all black-and-white striped moving objects. And slow things with spiny quills. Avoid all humans when they get into a feasting mood. Get near the tables fast, though, once the food is cooked. Stay close to their feet. Stay ready.
>
> But don't steal from their plates.
>
> Avoid medicine men. Snakes. Boys with BB guns. Anything rope-like or easily used to hang or tie. Avoid outhouse holes. Cats that live indoors. Do not sleep under cars. . . . Do not, unless you are absolutely certain you can blame it on a cat, eat any of their chickens. . . .
>
> Always, when in doubt, the rule is you are better off underneath the steps. Don't chase cars driven by young teenage boys. Don't chase cars driven by old ladies . . . Pee often. Take messages from tree stumps and corners of buildings.
>
> . . . Which is how I come to my next story of survival.[8]

The above is only a small excerpt of this section, all of which is incredibly funny for any reader, but especially for those readers who are familiar with the lives of reservation dogs.

Maybe more incredible to some than the humor itself, is that Erdrich was able to write this passage, to exhibit this much humor at what might have been the lowest point in her life. People who have been through great trauma usually have one of three reactions—some completely fall apart emotionally and physically and may even need to be hospitalized. Others find some deep well of fortitude and through luck and sheer strength of will survive and sometimes prosper. Yet a third group embodies elements of both despair and resilience. There is no evidence that Erdrich suffered any great overwhelming tragedies in her early life from which she might have learned coping mechanisms. She seemed to have had the kind of life that most people experience—a smooth progression with the inevitable blips on the radar of life, perhaps a failing grade on a school exam, or the illness of friends and family, or the death of pets, but no single terrifyingly horrible event. Many people who have led such ordinary lives or even charmed lives with every advantage often fall apart when a hurricane, real or metaphorical, descends upon them. Another American Indian writer, Sherman Alexie (Spokane/Coeur d'Alene) used a violent storm as a metaphor for a horrible family situation in "Every Little Hurricane."[9] Why was Erdrich still able to think and write with such humor? It may be cultural.

While there is little that is laughable in more than 500 years of colonialism of American Indians, the ability to laugh, even in the face of insurmountable difficulties, is useful for survival. Vine Deloria, Jr, is widely acknowledged as the person who raised awareness of the American Indian situation through such publications as *Custer Died For Your Sins*.[10] His works inspired the activism of the American Indian Movement in the late 1960s and the 1970s, and he was instrumental in the founding of American Indian or Native American Studies programs at major U.S. colleges and universities, including the American Indian Studies Program at the University of Arizona. Deloria has written extensively about American Indian humor. In a chapter on the subject in *Custer Died for Your Sins,* he wrote:

> Laughter encompasses the limits of the soul. In humor life is redefined and accepted. Irony and satire provide much keener insights into a group's collective psyche and values than do years of research.
>
> . . . Indians have found a humorous side of nearly every problem and the experiences of life have in general been so well defined through jokes and stories that they have become a thing unto themselves. . . .
>
> Humor has come to occupy such a prominent place in national Indian affairs that any kind of movement is impossible without it. . . .
>
> The more desperate the problem, the more humor is directed to describe it. Satirical remarks often circumscribe problems so that possible solutions are drawn from the circumstances that would not make sense if presented in other than a humorous form. . . . When a people can laugh at themselves and laugh at others and hold all aspects of life together without letting anybody drive them to extremes, then it seems to me that that people can survive.[11]

While Erdrich may not have had any one single tragic event in her own life prior to the separation from Dorris (which is not meant to discount the death of adopted son, Abel), she is American Indian of the Anishinaabe community. She would have grown up hearing the metanarratives of tragedy and loss for American Indians: The Trail of Tears, when entire American Indian tribes, notably the Cherokee, were forcefully removed from their homelands east of the Mississippi River and relocated to Oklahoma, and the broken treaties and lies that led to such events as the Minnesota Sioux uprising, which resulted in the largest mass execution in American history presided over by none other than

President Abraham Lincoln, and a multitude of other horrific events. Just as African Americans are aware of their history of slavery and repression, American Indians from childhood are taught the stories of tragedy that school history books have largely ignored or elided. Erdrich may have felt that if American Indians could survive and even prosper after 500 years of genocide, then she, as an Indian person, could survive her personal tragedy.

Because books take time to write and to go through the editing process, the publishing date always reflects work done earlier, usually a year or two previously, which means that the bulk of material in this book was likely written after the Erdrich–Dorris separation and before his suicide. One of the main characters in the book, Richard Whiteheart Beads, attempts suicide through carbon monoxide poisoning. He shuts himself in his truck in a closed garage with the motor running, but is distracted, gives up the effort, and leaves his truck running. However, one of his daughters, thinking that her father is going someplace, hides herself behind the pickup seat. Hoping to surprise him, she dies instead of Richard. Later on in the novel, Richard attempts suicide several times on the day that his ex-wife, Rozina, is getting married to another man. Erdrich constructs Richard's character as a publicly charming, politically aware man who always finds a scapegoat for his own transgressions. He is a selfish, egocentric man. Knowing the personal history of the Erdrich–Dorris relationship, it is tempting to draw parallels between Richard Whiteheart Beads and Michael Dorris. Certainly, Erdrich could not have known that Dorris would succeed in a suicide attempt as Richard ultimately does in the novel, but even the reactions of Rozina, Richard's wife, seem parallel to Erdrich's own. Rozina cannot live with Richard, and is filing for divorce when Richard first attempts suicide. Years later, after Richard does ultimately commit suicide, Rozina's response is withdrawal. She returns to her family home on the reservation, engages in the tradition of bead-working and spends time with her remaining living daughter and other family members, which is also similar to Erdrich's life after Dorris.

Erdrich could not have predicted that her life would come to resemble the novel she was writing, but years of living with Dorris's depression and suicidal thoughts and expressions were obviously an influence on her writing. As all creative writing students are told, write what you know, and it would seem that she did, including her construction of the character Richard Whiteheart Beads and his wife Rozina. That the character of Richard was Michael Dorris would not have been obvious to the friends and acquaintances who refused to accept Dorris as the haunted, suicidal man who was often violent with his children and who exerted a controlling influence over his wife and her work. If the Erdrich–Dorris marriage breakup had proceeded without any of the additional drama provided by the children's accusations of abuse, perhaps the divorce would have been granted, both Erdrich and Dorris would have continued as respected writers apart, and Louise might never have revisited those public claims of undying love and respectful collaboration that had been so much an attribute of their marriage.

For years after Dorris's death, Erdrich resisted openly discussing not only his suicide, but also the facts of their marriage. Only in 2010 in the interview for *Paris Review,* did she speak at length on these painful subjects. Interviewer Lisa Halliday asked Erdrich how the experience of writing *The Crown of Columbus* with Dorris was different from the experiences of writing her other books. Erdich opened up at last, with this:

> I've not spoken much about what it was like to work with Michael, partly because I feel that there's something unfair about it. He can't tell his side of the story. I have everything that we once had together. . . . it's difficult to set the record straight because it would be my view, the way I see it. Still, he controlled the narrative when he was living. I am weary of all the old leftover assumptions, and what else, really, do people have to go on?
>
> I would have loved for Michael to have had his own life as a writer and not covet my life as a writer. But he couldn't help himself. So in agreeing to write *The Crown of Columbus* I really made a deal, at least in my thoughts, that if we wrote this new book together, then we could openly work separately—as we always did in truth, of course.[12]

Here, then is the answer to that question so many had posed in the past: Did they really collaborate on all the work they published under their own individual names? The answer from Erdrich is "No." Of course, no writer ever works alone, even if their name appears singly on the cover. Writers do ask other people for advice as a manuscript is produced; sometimes, those people directly read drafts, sometimes not. Sometimes one or more people actively read a draft penciling suggestions and comments in the margins; then the manuscript may go to an agent who makes his or her own editorial comments, and from there to the publisher, where one or more editors do it all again. The ideas, the basic structure of a novel, and the style are uniquely the author's, but often, the final product is a far cry from the original work. Yet the person who came up with the original idea and wrote down the story is the person whose name appears on the book. Acknowledgement pages in books are full of thanks to many people, and in some cases these thanks run on for three or four pages. None of these people, however, would claim equal collaboration with the author as Dorris did to Erdrich. Here was a man who had talent of his own, yet could not allow his wife credit for her own unique stand-alone ability. Why did Erdrich allow him to take part of the credit that he had earned no more than any other author's editor? In the interview with Halliday, Erdrich goes on to say,

> I wanted to make him happy you know. He was the kind of person whom people want to make happy. People did this all the time, they tried to make him happy, but there was a deep impossibility within him and he couldn't really be happy. Or he couldn't be happy alone.[13]

Erdrich loved this man, so she tried to please him, but it would seem that the more she pleased him, the more he demanded. By all accounts, she was a shy person from her earliest childhood, not outspoken but passive except on the page. Early on in their marriage, she had become hostage to his demands, his rages, and found it difficult to break the cycle. How could she, when they had both publicly announced their undying love and their collaboration on everything they did? She thought that she could "ease" him out of the collaboration part, if not the marriage. She believed that writing one book jointly where both their names appeared on the cover would satisfy him, and then they could both be free to write as individuals. Obviously she felt smothered by his constant attention and, although she does not explicit say so, she resented his claims to her work. She stated,

> So I'd had the idea for *The Crown of Colombus;* I'd done the research and I said, this is the project. We can do it together because you can write your part and I can write mine and both of our names will be on the cover.
>   . . . I hoped that *The Crown of Columbus* would be what Michael needed in order to say, Now it is enough, we truly collaborated. Instead, it became the beginning of what he wanted for every book. When he told me he wanted both of our names on every book now, something in me—the writer, I guess—couldn't bear it any longer and that was the beginning of the long ending. . . .[14]

It was at this point that Erdrich moved her writing space from their main house in New Hampshire to the cottage across the road. *The Bingo Palace,* published in 1994, was likely a book that she had already done most of the work on with Dorris looking over her shoulder, so to speak, and possibly she also did some work on *Tales of Burning Love* (published in 1996) under Dorris's scrutiny as well. However, the subjects for her writing projects for the remaining years that they were together (*The Blue Jay's Dance,* the story of pregnancy and a child's first year of life from the point of view of the mother, herself, and the children's story, *Grandmother's Pigeon*) were subjects as distant from Dorris as could have been possible at the time.

Interviewer Halliday probes deeper and Erdrich, rather than withdraw from difficult questions as she had done for the previous 13 years, responded,

> Interviewer: Why do you think he wanted and needed so badly to see himself as a writer?
>   Erdrich: Perhaps because I loved writing so much and he loved me. Perhaps because he was a very good writer. Or perhaps—I don't say this in a negative or judgmental way, because this is the case with writers whether they admit it or not—Michael also adored everything that went on with the identity. He adored meeting other writers, adored being part of a literary world. He would answer everyone who wrote to him, beautiful letters, every single person. I don't take much pleasure in being "the writer."[15]

In the above, Erdrich is describing the two types of writer, the introvert and the extrovert, and it is easy to decide which was Dorris and which was Erdrich. Some writers, such as Hemingway, are able to closet themselves away to do the solitary work of writing, but only for a set amount of time. They need social interaction and crave the attention that comes with being a successful writer. For them, writing and publishing is a means to the end of getting positive feedback. Dorris was this type.

The other kind of writer prefers solitude, the time they spend alone filling an empty page. For them, writing is an end unto itself, and the attention that comes with successful publication is something that must be endured rather than sought and enjoyed. These people go to book signing parties because they must but sneak glances at the clock to see if enough time has passed so they can leave. Erdrich is this type. Of course, not all writers fall neatly into one category or the other. There are writers who are somewhere in between, and writers who may be introverts part of the time, and extroverts at other times.

A marriage between an extrovert and an introvert can certainly work. Sometimes one fulfills the other, and this may be what Erdrich and Dorris had in the beginning, but as time passed, the extrovert began to assume control. There are gardeners who have set Pampas grass in their yard where it flourished, but then to the gardener's dismay, the grass self-seeded and began to take over, smothering out all the other plants until it had to be removed before it killed everything else in the garden.

In the Halliday interview, Erdrich says that she allowed Dorris to continue taking over her career. She said,

> There were signs from the beginning, but I ignored them or even exhaustedly encouraged them. . . . Actually, I was tired. *Love Medicine* and *Jacklight* were published in 1984, and I had a baby. *The Beet Queen* was published in 1985, and I bore my second daughter that year. What kind of woman can do that? A tired woman who lets her husband do the talking because she has the two best things—the babies and the writing. Yet at some point the talking infected the writing. I looked into the mirror and I saw Michael. I began to write again in secret and put together a novel that I didn't show him.[16]

Perhaps that novel was *The Antelope Wife.*

The reviews for this novel stand in stark contrast to the tepid or even harsh criticism that *The Crown of Columbus* earned. Writing for *The New York Times*, reviewer Michiko Kakutani, who had written less than ecstatically about *The Crown of Columbus*, wrote enthusiastically, but with cautions to readers about *The Antelope Wife*. Kakutani urges Erdrich's readers to avoid looking for parallels between Erdrich's personal life and the plot of *The Antelope Wife*. Kakutani argues that all writers' works arise from their own personal experiences, so similarities between the story and the writer's personal life is inevitable. Kakutani believes that this novel is a "virtuoso" display of Erdrich's prodigious writing skills, and that is all that needs to be said about the book.[17]

Erdrich had proved to her readers and to literary critics that she was a talented writer in her own right, that she did not need Dorris's "collaborative" or editorial efforts, but could do very well without his influence. Her next book,

The Last Report of the Miracles at Little No Horse would not come out until 2001, but the three years between these two books would be full, rewarding ones for Erdrich.

NOTES

1. Louise Erdrich, *Books and Islands in Ojibwe Country* (Washington, D.C.: National Geographic Society, 2003), 22.

2. Staff writer, "Wife Claims Dorris Was Suicidal For Years: Only She Knew of His Tormented Secret," *Seattle Post-Intelligencer,* April 19, 1997.

3. Louise Erdrich, *The Antelope Wife* (New York: HarperFlamingo an imprint of HarperCollins: 1998), 4.

4. Louise Erdrich, *Tracks* (New York: HarperCollins: 1988), 110.

5. The man in the story sells his pocket watch to buys combs for his lover's beautiful hair, but she sells her hair to buy a fob for his watch.

6. Lorena L. Stookey, *Louise Erdrich: A Critical Companion* (Westport: Greenwood Press, 1999), 134.

7. Ibid., 15, 20–21, 24, 26, 29, 37. 39, 45, 52–53, 83, 94, 113, 124–25, 134, 139.

8. Erdrich, *The Antelope Wife,* 79–80.

9. Sherman Alexie, "Every Little Hurricane," in *Lone Ranger and Tonto Fistfight in Heaven* (New York: HarperPerennial, 1993), 1.

10. Vine Deloria, Jr., *Custer Died for Your Sins: An Indian Manifesto* (New York: McMillan Publishing Co., 1969).

11. Ibid., 146–7, 167.

12. Lisa Halliday, "The Art of Fiction No. 208," *Paris Review* No. 195 (Winter, 2010): 158.

13. Ibid.

14. Ibid., 158–59.

15. Ibid., 159.

16. Ibid., 160.

17. Michiko Kakutani, "*Antelope Wife:* Myths of Redemption Amid a Legacy of Loss," *Book of the Times, The New York Times,* March 24, 1998.

SIX

Miracles, Birchbark, and Prestidigitation

When you come to the end of a section of your life, you do not consciously start the rest of your life with a new plan, a change of direction, or a goal in mind. You live day by day, doing the little things that are necessary—making the bed, brushing your teeth, getting the children off to school, buying a loaf of bread at the grocery store. Eventually out of those mundane events, something comes along. For most of us, it is something simple such as a job where we exercise a long-disused skill or going back to school to learn a new skill. We meet new people or renew old acquaintances so that day by day, the monochromatic grays of depression and loss take on the colors of life. At first, those colors are pastels—pale greens and yellows and pinks—as if we lived in a dimly lit room circumscribed by circumstances. For those of us who are lucky, someone or something turns up the light until now and then a vibrant red or green or blue catches our eye. We turn toward it, greedily, clutching it and nurturing it and hoping that it will bear fruit.

At the age of 44, when *The Antelope Wife* was published, Erdrich already had a considerable body of work behind her, and the riches of family and culture as well, but there were many years left for her to live and work and thrive. The color may have begun to return to her life in 1999, when she published her second children's book, *The Birchbark House*. Her first children's book, *Grandmother's Pigeon*, was published in 1996, when her three oldest daughters, except for Madeline, were all 12 years old or less, and that first children's book earned ecstatic reviews. The second children's book was dedicated to daughter

Persia, and she thanks this daughter on the Acknowledgments page and says that this book and others to follow are an attempt to retrace her family history.

School children are often introduced to early pioneer life in America through the books of Laura Ingalls Wilder. Erdrich's books recall that same time period, but from the perspective of an American Indian (Ojibwe) child, Omakayas. Erdrich herself created little drawings, vignettes that illustrate the story. Well-received by the reading public as well as the critics, the book earned a finalist position for the National Book Award.

Another event that cheered Erdrich during the difficult years following the sexual abuse scandal and suicide of her husband began when she noticed a boarded-up storefront in Minneapolis on West 21st Street. It had once been a butcher shop, had last been a dentist's office but had been closed for years. Erdrich and her sister, Heid, decided to buy it together and start a business selling books and native arts. They named the business Birchbark Books and Native Arts, maybe for the successful children's book, but also because birch bark plays a prominent role in the Erdrich sisters' Ojibwe culture. This tree bark was traditionally used to make houses and lightweight canoes, but also serving platters, plates, and trays for winnowing wild rice, a staple of the Ojiba diet, and even decorative items with designs bitten (yes, bitten by the artist's teeth) into the wood. The work to get the old building in shape was daunting. The website for Birchbark Books and Native Arts states,

> We are proud of our original wooden floor, which belonged to the meat market this once was. It took an enormous amount of volunteer effort to pry up two layers of plywood, three of linoleum, and one of tarpaper and then to extract thousands of nails from the boards underneath. The result is very weathered and uneven, but the real thing.[1]

The centerpiece of the store is a Catholic confessional booth that Erdrich found in an architectural salvage store. Heid had suggested that they use it as a listening booth for CDs and tapes, while Erdrich's mother thought it would be a good place to shelve books on sin. Ultimately, the confessional is decoration, but a framed copy of the 1837 treaty with the Ojibwe is housed inside, an ironic statement about who has sinned against whom. A canoe hangs from the ceiling. The store sells native arts and crafts as well as books.

Opened in July of 2000, more than 12 years later, the store is still operating next door to the Kenwood Café, which gets an advertising plug on the bookstore's website. In a time when small, privately owned bookstores are being driven out of business by big box bookstores, online sites, and e-books, it is a miracle that Birchbark is thriving. The store's success can be, of course, partly because one of the owners, Louise Erdrich, is a phenomenally successful writer, and the other owner, sister Heid, is a talented writer herself, if somewhat less commercially successful.

Louise does not run the store herself, but has delegated those responsibilities to Heid and to a staff of competent and hardworking people. The store is also an arts center that has hosted literary events over the years. Such native authors as Ada Deer, Joy Harjo, Thomas King, Jim Northrup, and John Trudell have all presented their work at the store and left their autographs. While the bookstore was being renovated and opened, Erdrich discovered a disconcerting fact.

At the age of 46, she was pregnant again. The father was Tobasonakwuk, an Ojibwe traditional healer. When and how and where they met and the history of their romance is something Erdrich has never divulged. The child, another girl, was born in 2000 and named Azure according to interviewer, Karen Olson.[2] However, when this author asked the names of her children, Erdrich gave the child's Anishinaabe name, Nenaa'ikiizhikok. It may be that Azure is the English translation of the Anishinaabe word. Considering the public scrutiny that Erdrich and her daughters endured over the accusations against Dorris and his subsequent suicide, Erdrich's reluctance to give any information about this last child and the child's father is understandable and even laudable. The two things she values most in her life are her family and her writing, in that order of priority.

While she was pregnant with her last child and busy with the bookstore renovations and opening, she was also doing what she always does—writing. One result of that work was published in 2001, *The Last Report of the Miracles at Little No Horse,* which brought back characters from her earlier novels, *Tracks, Love Medicine,* and *The Bingo Palace.* Erdrich said that this is a book that she had begun back in 1988, so it may be the novel that she kept secret from Michael Dorris. According to Karen Olson, Erdrich,

> . . . originally intended it to explain how all the earlier novels came into being. She imagined the local priest in Argus, Father Damien, who had appeared as a minor character in *Love Medicine* [and in *Tracks*], divulging all the confessions of the community to a writer who would turn out to be Erdrich herself. It wasn't until six years and several books later that Erdrich picked up *The Last Report* again.[3]

The book resuscitates what is arguably the most fascinating character that Erdrich ever created, the woman who started out as Pauline Puyat and became the nun, Sister Leopoldo. Pauline, a native woman who denied her heritage in order to be accepted as a nun, was one of the two alternating voices in *Tracks.* Most readers feel sympathy for the character early in the book when she declares herself to be so plain and unnoticeable as to disappear in comparison with the striking main character of Fleur. However, readers' patience and sympathy quickly wane when it becomes obvious that Pauline is a devious liar, jealous of others, and willing to commit almost any evil act for revenge while declaring her own piety. She takes her vows and becomes Sister Leopoldo in *Tracks,* but the character was too juicy, too uniquely evil to let go. *The Last Report of the Miracles at Little No Horse* is also about Father Damien, a woman who has disguised her female identity and lived as a priest for 50 years, and about a church investigator sent out to document the life of Sister Leopoldo when she is being considered for sainthood, which seems a bizarre consideration for most readers who are privy to Sister Leopoldo's dark evil secrets.

The book opens with Agnes DeWitt, a woman left distraught, confused, and directionless after her lover's death. Agnes met a priest who was traveling to a new assignment among the Anishinaabe and had been intrigued by his missionary status and his lack of enthusiasm for his new assignment. After both Agnes and the priest are swept away in a flood, Agnes discovers the dead priest's body and assumes his identity.

While such transgendered people are not readily accepted in dominant American society, traditional American Indian societies have not only accepted them, but honored them. Two-spirited is the term used by many American Indian tribes, which is not meant to imply a sexual binary, but rather, a range of sexual identification, expression, and gender specific social roles. Mainstream culture has suppressed two-spirited people, but many American Indian groups maintained or have more recently revived gender designations that go beyond male/female. Among American Indians, males and females each have a single spirit at their center, but transgendered, lesbian, gay, or bisexual people have two spirits, hence the origin of the two-spirit term. Trickster figures such as coyote, rabbit, raven, or spider, are magical, mystical creatures that transgress boundaries of ethics, time, and space, and even the boundaries of gender.

In *Little No Horse,* Erdrich constructs the character of Agnes/Father Damien as a White person rather than an American Indian, which allows the character more anguished internal, sometimes doubting thoughts than if the character had been American Indian because Father Damien/Agnes does not come from a society that readily accepts transgendered people. It takes an effort of will for Father Damien to carry on and accept her/himself as the male priest as well as an effort to seem entirely male to other characters. She must be aware of and practice those physical gestures that hint to gender, as well as learn to conceal her monthly menstrual flow. She is a two-spirited person who cannot openly declare her sexually, but is forced to conceal it within the boundaries of dominant society, a Catholic society that has declared any gender expression other than all male or all female as being anathema before the Christian God.

While Father Damien is successful in disguising his female body for most of the other characters within the story, it is not so for some others, particularly the two priests, Father Gregory and Father Jude. However, when Father Jude has a sudden insight into the true nature of Father Damien's sexuality, he dismisses it with the notion that perhaps Damien has a twin sister that Jude may have met before, blinding himself to reality within the acceptable context of Catholicism. However, when Father Gregory discovers the female body of Damien, he falls in love with her and urges her to run away with him, but Agnes demurs saying, "I cannot leave who I am."[4] Gregory and Damien's affair introduces the possibility that Agnes/Damien is not a person transgendered by internal sexual imperative, but is really a woman who masquerades as a man to overcome the impossible life situation in which she found herself, or yet a third possibility—that Agnes/Damien is bisexual. All of these possibilities and more are acceptable within traditional American Indian societies, but not usually—at least not at the time setting of the story—within mainstream society and certainly not within the dogma of Catholicism. Here again, readers see Erdrich working out her own complex and sometimes conflicting spiritual indoctrination within the context of fiction.

These issues of social acceptance or rejection of lesbian, gay, transgendered, or bisexual people were in the forefront of political discussions in the United States before, during, and after the time *Last Report* was published and continue to be hot button topics. Deirdre Keenan wrote that Erdrich's work:

> . . . cannot provide a panacea for the gender troubles in mainstream culture. It is fiction, after all. . . . In the current political struggles between those who advocate for lesbian, gay, bisexual, and transgender rights and those who would amend suppressive and exclusive legislation, Native American Two Spirit traditions—whether represented in fiction or nonfiction—could mediate a vision where all individuals' gender identities and sexualities could be honored.[5]

Early excerpts published in *The New Yorker* magazine created interest in the eventual book publication, and the publisher advertised the book in promotional ads. When the book was released, Erdrich went on a book tour, of course. Book of the Month Club and Quality Paperback Book Club both made this novel one of their selections. Most of the reviews were excellent using such words as "beguiling" (*New York Times Book Review*), "heartfelt" (*Los Angeles Times*), and "spellbinding" (*Elle*). The *Los Angeles Times* reviewer wrote, "Messy, ribald, deeply tragic, preposterous and heartfelt," adding, "*The Last Report of the Miracles at Little No Horse* is a love story, and what shines most brilliantly through its pages are Erdrich's intelligence and compassion."[6] If anyone thought that *The Antelope Wife* might have been a fluke, that Erdrich's writing without Dorris might not be of the same quality as her earlier collaborative work with him, this novel certainly ended that speculation for good. Not all the reviews of *Little No Horse* were completely complimentary; none ever are. For example, the headline for a review by Mark Schechner printed in the New York *Buffalo News* reads—"Erdrichland Suffers a Surfeit of Characters, Plots."[7] The headline is, however, more than a little deceptive for the bulk of the article is complimentary. Schechner continued with, ". . . Erdrich remains a formidable talent, indeed, a force whom nothing deters."[8] The review praises with faint damnation, not entirely a bad situation for Erdrich.

Of course, Erdrich had other works in progress, including another children's book that would be published the following year in 2002, *The Range Eternal*. Not about land, as one might expect, the story is about a different kind of "range," a stove used for both heating and cooking, which is at the heart of the home where the young main character lives. Only 32 pages in length, this book aimed at a younger audience than her first two children's books, perhaps because Erdrich now had a very young child.

Even parents who are not writers sometimes make up original stories to tell their children at bedtime when the classic stories of Dr. Seuss become too well-worn. This story may have begun as one Erdrich made up for Nenaa-ikiizhikok (Kiizhikok for short). Rather than black and white drawings, this one has colorful paintings as illustrations, but Erdrich left that task to others. She was busy, after all, with a baby to care for, a house, the bookstore, her extended family of parents, brothers and sisters and their families, and more novels that she continued to work on and that would see publication in the next few years. But there was a nonfiction book that would come out next, before any more novels or children's books: *Books and Islands in Ojibwe Country*.[9]

When Kiizkikok was 18 months old, Erdrich packed the baby into her blue van and took a road trip up to Lake of the Woods in Canada where she, Kiizhikok, and the child's father canoed to several islands and cultural sites over the course of several days. From there, Erdrich and the child traveled in the van to an island on Rainy Lake, where a long deceased former woodsman and wanderer and collector of books named Ernest Oberholtzer had lived with his Ojibwe friends and collected more than 11,000 books, which are still housed there in his main residence and other outbuildings on the property.

The confluence of these two ideas—islands and books—provides the title for this nonfiction book, in which Erdrich opens up her life to the public in a way she had never done before. She writes in small statements that allow glimpses into her life without revealing much background behind those enigmatic comments. She is like the exotic dancer Sally Rand with her feather fan, promising to reveal all, but revealing very little. The personal statements and glimpses into her real life beneath and behind her books are scattered here and there, but most of the first two-thirds of the book contains historical and cultural information about the islands that she, Kiizhikok, and Tobasonakwuk visit by boat. Erdrich lyrically describes the natural landscape—the trees, the lakes, the wild plants from which medicine can be made, and the animals that inhabit these places. The book also contains descriptions of ancient rock paintings and pictograms and more recent ruins of abandoned human habitation, including the place where Tobasonakwuk was born.

Gradually, she reveals a little of Tobasonakwuk's life. He is a spiritual healer, a medicine man who conducts sweat lodge ceremonies and supervises petitioners who undertake a four-day retreat for a vision quest. His practice is spiritual, to be respected as much as the Christian pastor who leads and guides a church full of parishioners, but vastly different from the minister or priest. While the priest or the pastor usually has a salary paid by the church and is provided with a comfortable place to live, sometimes even a car and an expense account, a native medicine man has no such economic bulwark. Nor does the traditional medicine man own or rent a lavish lodge in a scenic location, where he conducts "authentic" ceremonies for wealthy or at least upper-middle class White people who want an alternative spiritual experience and can afford to pay thousands of dollars for the privilege.

Medicine men such as Tobasonakwuk, and sometimes medicine women, rarely take money for their spiritual guidance. Rather, they are given offerings—always tobacco, and often ordinary food items such as three-pound cans of coffee, flour, sugar, canned goods, or household goods such as blankets and sheets and towels. Money offerings are frowned upon but have become more necessary in a capitalist society, where the rent and the utility bills cannot be paid for with a blanket or a can of coffee. It is a difficult life that will never bring riches or fame, only the satisfaction of being of use to people who suffer pain, seek guidance for some important decision, or wish to offer thanks to the spirit world for some boon that they have been granted. If it is a difficult life for the medicine man practitioner, it is even more so for a woman who chooses to love and live with such a person and bear his children. (Most spiritual practitioners are men. Women who choose to become medicine persons usually do so later in life, when their children are grown.)

Mary Brave Bird has written frankly about what it is like to be the partner of a medicine man in both *Lakota Woman* and *Ohitka Woman*.[10] While there are moments of spiritual wonder, there are also great difficulties because the wife of a medicine man must share her husband with whomever is in need, and those in need do not show up for appointments on a 9–5 schedule such as a doctor's patients. They may come at 2:00 a.m.; they may come with a dozen relatives; they may come drunk; they may bring children who must be cared for, and everyone must be fed and found sleeping places out of the cold or the heat or the rain. Mary Crow Dog/Brave Bird was unable to endure this life and eventually left her medicine man/partner, Crow Dog. His spiritual practice continues mostly in the upper Midwest states of South Dakota, Nebraska, and Minnesota, although he does travel to other locations around the country and the world from time to time. He has formed domestic partnerships and marriages with other women through the years, some of whom have been able to tolerate and even thrive with him and his unusual spiritual calling.

Erdrich's relationship with Tobasonakwuk probably survives because they live separately for most of the year; she in Minneapolis with her daughters, her writing, and her bookstore, while he continues his spiritual practice and his other work in tribal governance in Canada. An online blog states:

> Tobasonakwuk Kinew is an esteemed member of the University of Winnipeg community in his multiple roles as Elder and Faculty for the Indigenous Governance department and Master's in Developmental practice with a focus on [the] Indigenous Development program.[11]

The above information indicates that Tobasonakwuk probably has an income over and above what might be provided by his spiritual practice. There is no information in Erdrich's book about how or when she met Tobasonakwuk. It is impossible to know if he visits in Minneapolis or if they only meet when Erdrich travels to Canada. It would seem from the sketchy information available, that they spend most of their lives living separately. Some people need the constant presence of another person, to live so close they almost breathe through the same straw, but that is the life Erdrich had with Dorris, which ended so badly. Tobasonakwuk is there as an anchor for her life and for

Kiizhikok, but they do not need to dance attendance upon each other. He would never tell her that a character in one of her stories is inauthentic or needs further development, and she would never tell him the proper way to conduct a vision quest ceremony. They each accept and support their individual passions without interference from the other.

On her trip north to visit the islands of Lake of the Woods with Tobasonakwuk, Erdrich was not even sure where she would find him. She writes, "They [her brothers] ask about him and about my plans for this trip. I am forced to say that, as usual, I have no exact idea how I'll actually meet up with him. Although, as always, I am sure it will happen."[12] The book details and emphasizes shared experiences between Erdrich and Tobasonakwuk that all humans need in order to build a common history of living and loving, such as the moment when they see a sturgeon leap from the lake.

All of a sudden between our boat and the fringed woods a great fish vaults up into the air. . . . The fish I just saw was not a muskie. It was even bigger. Tobasonakwuk sees it from the corner of his eye and slows the boat down.
   "Asema," he says, and puts the tobacco in the water. That fish was the *nameh*. The sturgeon. Tobasonakwuk is happy and moved to see it because, he says, "They rarely show themselves like that."[13]

The book also offers moments of tender concern for each other, such as a point in their boat trip when Erdrich attempts a climb up a rock face to see a thunderbird rock painting and to leave a tobacco offering. She gives up because the path to the painting is broken by an open space with a steep drop. Tobasonakwuk undertakes the climb in her place, and returns after successfully leaving the tobacco offering in front of the painting. She is dismayed, and as she puts it, "just a little pissed off." He tells her that he got there by jumping, and she responds, "You could have broken your leg!" He demurs that it isn't the 15 feet that she insists it is, but more like six feet. She says, "Don't ever do that again!" As they travel on, she muses about his "stubborn-headed insistence that he's still a young man." Finally, she says, "You've got to quit doing things like this," but then acknowledges that her words "will have no effect, and besides, this is one of the reasons I love him. He's a little crazy, in a good way, half teenager and half *akiwenzii*."[14]

The last part of this book recounts Erdrich's visit to the island on Rainy Lake just across the border in Canada from International Falls, Minnesota. As an Ojibwe person, a writer, and lover of books, she is, of course, fascinated with the place where Oberholtzer spent most of his life under semi-primitive conditions in the wild while collecting a wide variety of books, from Keats, and Shakespeare, and Walt Whitman to volumes on sexuality. On the island, she examines and reads parts of the books, but also interacts with some unique people who live nearby, who care for the books and the property and share her love of the place.

Back home in Minneapolis, she is faced immediately with death, not of a human but of a living being. One of the old trees in her yard—the one she named Old Stalwart—has been condemned by the city as a victim of Dutch Elm disease and must be destroyed. Erdrich grieves for the tree, and as it falls, a reader cannot help but be reminded of one of the final scenes in *Tracks,* where Fleur has sawed partly through the trunks of the trees around her house so that when the lumber company arrives to remove her from the property, she cast a spell to bring the trees down to kill or injure the usurpers. No one dies when Old Stalwart comes down, but the sense of sadness and loss is palpable in Erdrich's words,

> . . . I watch it go, with Kiizhikok, and feel the shock of its passage, a resounding shudder of the earth that tingles in our feet. That's it. It is gone. This has been a warm winter and a record number of elms have succumbed, as the deep cold helps kill off the beetles that spread the sickness. As I am finishing this book, the city stump grinder arrives, and by the end of the day his rotary blade has turned the rest of Old Stalwart into a pile of chips. It will be another hundred years, if the house survives this long, before a tree grown in its place tops the roofline and teases the sky.[15]

This book is a travelogue that charts a circular journey from Minneapolis to Canada and back again, but also a journey though a few weeks of Erdrich's life that may reveal more about her and in greater depth than all the interviews she ever gave, with or without Dorris. It is a gift freely given to her readers. A writer owes her readers a good story, fair value for the price of the book, but nothing more. However, most humans have an insatiable curiosity, as was demonstrated by the interest in the Erdrich–Dorris relationship after his suicide. Some readers want to know not only the story, but everything about the person who created the story. Here, Erdrich offers some biographical information, but only what she is comfortable revealing. Much is left to the imagination, like Sally Rand with her fan, and just like the fan, in this book, Erdrich misdirects the eye, so now you see it—or think you see it—and now you do not. Some entertainers—musicians, writers, artists—thrive on attention, need it to fuel their work as much as they need air, water, and food to sustain their bodies. Erdrich's work is fueled and sustained by her family and her heritage. Given her preferences, she would never give a single interview. Asked by one interviewer, "What single thing would improve the quality of your life?" she responded, "Not doing publicity." But, she does it, because, as she responded to the question, "What is the most important lesson life has taught you," she said, "There is always the need for some publicity."[16]

Erdrich had stretched her repertoire with *Books and Islands,* but she also published within her comfort zone in 2003 bringing out a book of poetry, *Original Fire,* and her eighth novel, *The Master Butcher's Singing Club.* As with her earlier novels, a portion of this one, too, had been previously published as a short story, "The Butcher's Wife," in *The New Yorker.* Interestingly, a poem with the same title was published in her first collection of poetry, *Jacklight,* back in 1984. This novel, too, got mostly good reviews, but *The New York Times* published one that praised and one that panned it. Michiko Kakutani, who had written glowingly about most of Erdrich's other works, praised this one as well, when she wrote—"[the novel is] emotionally resonant, [Erdrich displays] sheer authority as a storyteller, her instinctive sympathy for her characters, her energetic inventiveness, her effortless ability to connect public and private concerns." However, reviewer Brooke Allen, in the *New York Sunday Times* wrote that Erdrich's "lyrical gifts cannot always keep up with her soaring ambitions," criticized the characters as not believable, and called it "too disorganized, too unfocused, too wide-ranging to sustain much force."[17]

While this book is in her usual style, her subject matter and characters are somewhat different from earlier books. Most of the attention in her earlier novels is on her Anishinaabe heritage, with some nods to the German side of the family as in *The Beet Queen*. *The Master Butcher's Singing Club,* however, specifically honors Erdrich's German grandfather who immigrated to the United States in 1920 after fighting for Germany in World War I. This grandfather, Ludvig Erdrich, whose photo appears on the cover of the hardback edition, was a butcher. Erdrich states,

> He was an amazing human being. He worked slavishly in order to earn the money for his family to join him. My father idolized him—so although the character of Fidelis Waldvogel isn't my grandfather, I still wanted to write about someone like him, like the people who came to America and struggled so hard to survive.[18]

While the main character of the novel honors Erdrich's grandfather Ludvig, the plot of the story is an admixture of Ojibwa and German stories from both ethnicities of characters, such as Erdrich's own heritage. At 388 pages in the Harper Perennial edition, this is one of her longest, most ambitious books, almost as long as the novel jointly written with Dorris, *The Crown of Columbus*. Brooke Allen's comments that *The Master Butcher's Singing Club* suffers from a surfeit of characters is not without merit, but those who love Erdrich's work are willing to engage and grapple with the cast for the pleasure of Erdrich's poetic language and vivid descriptions of people and landscapes.

The poetry collection that was also published in 2003, *Original Fire*, is a return to the genre of her earlier writing roots. This book includes works previously published in *Jacklight* and *Baptism of Desire* with some new poems as well. These are not poems with classic rhyming patterns, but free verse. This is the kind of poetry she wrote in *Jacklight,* but the new poems in this third book of poetry eschew even informal free verse. These are narrative poems instead, much more in the style of native poet Adrian Louis. The title of this book is taken from the final section, all new poems, about pregnancy, childbirth, and mothering, where she writes about the "soft and original fire" in the beginning lives of her children.

Erdrich's writing career began with poetry, but poems were too small, too finite, to contain her epic, sweeping stories and complex characters that she elaborated upon within her novels. Once she had written the novels, she returned to those themes and ideas, here and there plucking out representative nuggets to represent in poetry. Of this third book of poetry, reviewer John Freeman wrote,

> What makes *Original Fire* so abundantly sexy is not its description of the act itself, but the way Erdrich weaves desire into themes of memory, home and history . . . Erdrich has sublimated the ferocity of her desire into parenthood, its watchfulness now tender and nurturing. These flames will no longer burn down the house. They will heat it.[19]

Most authors count it as a supreme accomplishment to write and publish one book every three or four years. From 2001–2003—in three years—Erdrich published five books, and three of those—*Books and Islands in Ojibwe Country, The Master Butcher's Singing Club,* and *Original Fire*—in one year, 2003. Further, most writers work in one genre: poetry or fiction (which can be broken into the two sub-genres of short story and novel), or creative nonfiction. Erdrich published three books in three different genres in one year, and all of them were successful, both commercially and critically. That in itself is some kind of miracle.

NOTES

1. Birchbark Books and Native Arts Store website, Birchbarkbooks.com/ourstory.
2. Karen Olson, *The Complicated Life of Louise Erdrich* (Barnes & Noble, 2001). An excerpt from this book is currently available on research website www.highbeam.com, but this author's searches have turned up no extant copies of the book.
3. Ibid.
4. Louise Erdrich, *The Last Report of the Miracles at Little No Horse* (New York: Harper Collins, 2001), 53.
5. Dierdre Keenan, "Unrestricted Territory: Gender, Two Spirits, and Louise Erdrich's *The Last Report of the Miracles at Little No Horse,*" *American Indian Culture and Research Journal* 30:2 (2006): 11.
6. Staff writer, Book Reviews, *The Last Report of the Miracles at Little No Horse. Los Angeles Times.* http://www.bookbrowse.com/reviews/index.cfm/book_number/792/the-last-report-of-the-miracles-at-little-no-horse.
7. Mark Schechner, "Erdrichland Suffers A Surfeit of Characters, Plots," *Buffalo News,* April 8, 2001.
8. Ibid.
9. Louise Erdrich, *Books and Islands in Ojibwe Country* (Washington, D.C.: National Geographic Society, 2003).
10. Mary Crow Dog, with Richard Erdoes, *Lakota Woman* (New York: Grove Press, 1990), and Mary Brave Bird, with Richard Erdoes, *Ohitika Woman* (New York: Grove Press, 1993). *Lakota Woman* was made into a movie in 1994, produced by TNT and Jane Fonda, starring Irene Bedard.
11. Ojibway Confessions, Rightojibway.blogspot.com/2011/10/tobasonakuk-peter-kinew-recieves.html (misspelling of "receives" original in the web reference).
12. Erdrich, *Books and Islands,* 23.
13. Ibid., 74–75.
14. Ibid., 69–70.

15. Ibid., 132.

16. Louise Erdrich, *The Master Butcher's Singing Club* (New York: HarperCollins, 2003), 5.

17. Quoted from Deborah Caulfield Rybak and Jon Tevlin, "Bookmarks: Erdrich Praises Estrogen," *Minneapolis Star Tribune,* February 16, 2003.

18. Erdrich, *The Master Butcher's Singing Club,* 6.

19. John Freeman, "POETRY: Passion still burns brightly in Erdrich's fiery poems," *Minneapolis Star Tribune,* September 7, 2003.

SEVEN

The Second Flowering

Over the next seven years, from 2004–2010, Erdrich wrote and published seven books, an average of one per year, not quite her record of three in one year, but still enough to turn other writers green with envy. The seven that she published were in three different genres: two more children's books, four more novels, and a collection of short stories.

Her writing consumed much of her time, but little is known of what else she did. Knowing her devotion to her children, much of her personal time must have been spent in tending to the needs of her youngest daughter, Kiizhikhok. Her other daughters were reaching for their own separate skies, but she encouraged them, supported them, and talked to them often on the telephone and in person. The oldest daughter, Persia, worked at the Birchbark Book Store, where Erdrich called in every day, if she did not actually appear in person. She has spoken often about the difficulty of learning the Ojibwe language of her mother, and her determination to persist, so she may have continued with that study during this period of her life. There would have been visits to Kiizhikok's father, visits to her parents, her brothers and sisters and their families at holidays and other times that were not necessarily holidays or marking family anniversaries, but just because she wanted that family connection. Bits of information about her writing and her life besides the writing leaked out here and there in interviews she gave at book signings and other events as each of her books were released by the publishers.

Four Souls[1] was the next book after *The Master Butcher's Singing Club,* the first of the seven in seven years. This book answers questions raised about what happened to the enigmatic character of Fleur at the end of *Tracks,* published back in 1988. Fleur Pillager, beautiful and strong, had struggled against all odds to preserve her land from being taken over by an unscrupulous timber baron, but when she failed, she loaded the grave markers of her family into a wheelbarrow and pushed it off, not into the sunset, but into the sunrise. Other novels, such as *Love Medicine,* offer glimpses of Fleur as an older woman returned to her home territory, living semi-wild and reclusive, but readers wondered about what happened in those in-between years.

Four Souls tells the story of Fleur in believable action as she travels to Minneapolis to seek vengeance upon the timber baron, John James Mauser, who stole her land. She takes a job as a laundress for Mauser's sister-in-law, manipulates her way into the Mauser family, and eventually marries the man that she despises and bears him an autistic child. While autism is not the same as Fetal Alcohol Syndrome, raising a special needs child is always difficult no matter what the diagnosis. It is easy to surmise that Erdrich's own experience of raising her three adopted special needs children must have influenced the characterization of the child in this novel. Erdrich's fans, including this author, were delighted to learn more details of Fleur Pillager's life, but for others who had not read *Tracks,* the plot and the character of Fleur may have seemed inaccessible. *Publishers Weekly* wrote:

> The themes of revenge and redemption are strong here, especially when combined with the pull of her lyrical prose; Erdrich may not ensnare many new readers, but she will certainly satisfy her already significant audience.[2]

This book, like *Tracks,* has multiple narrators who sometimes contradict each other in their telling of Fleur's story. Erdrich again keeps the character of Fleur enigmatic and distant by never letting Fleur tell her own story. Readers never know what Fleur truly thinks or believes about anything nor what she is planning to do next, they only know what others think of Fleur and her actions. In *Four Souls,* the narrators are Nanapush, one of the two narrators from *Tracks,* now a tribal official, and Margaret Kashpaw, Nanapush's wife who is now a strong woman in her own right. A third narrator is Polly, the unmarried sister-in-law of Mauser.

While the book is indeed about revenge and the price that must be paid for it, it is also full of humor and comic asides, as would be expected from the trickster figure of Nanapush. In her review of the novel, Carole Goldberg states that although revenge is the theme of the novel, the cost is high, particularly for Fleur. Nanapush, too, seeks revenge at great risk. Goldberg continues with, "Another author might have exhausted her material long ago,"[3] but insists that the characters Erdrich has created continue to delight her readers.

"Inexhaustible" could very well be an adjective used to describe Erdrich herself. In 2005, she published *The Game of Silence,* which continues the children's story she began with the publication of *The Birchbark House.* The main character in both is Omakayas, an Ojibwe word meaning "little frog." Erdrich also illustrated this one herself with pencil drawings that must have delighted her to draw. The back of the book contains additional material—a map of Omakayas's adventures during the game of silence as well as a family tree for the character. Extra pages tell young (and old!) readers how to create their own family tree. This was undoubtedly created by Erdrich herself and not someone at the publishing house because the directions, especially the last paragraph, are so clearly in her own voice. She wrote, "Have fun! This is your chance to discover how everyone is related and teach the rest of your family about their own history."[4] Those words "everyone is related" are typical of native philosophy in the Upper Great Plains and elsewhere in the United States. Many native speeches and writings from tribes of the region end with the words, *Mitakuye Oyasin,* almost an invocation, a prayer that the preceding words will bring honor rather than shame upon the speaker or author's family. The words are Lakota (Sioux) rather than Ojibwe in origin, but commonly used by other tribes. The exact translation is something like "all my relations," but the meaning is that we are all related, and should be respectful of each other as if we were family.

Within the dedication, inside back cover notes, and a personal letter to the readers, Erdrich offers tiny glimpses into her personal life. The book is dedicated to her third daughter, Aza, who had been included in group dedications to her children before, but never one just for her. With daughter Persia actively involved in her mother's life through the bookstore, and youngest daughter Kiizhikok needing so much attention, perhaps Erdrich felt that she needed to pay special tribute to one of her middle children.

The letter to the reader brings to mind the letters that Ralph Erdrich wrote to his daughter at Dartmouth, but for a younger reader. It is newsy and witty and fun. It reads in part,

> I began writing *The Game of Silence* while I was still writing *The Birchbark House,* on Madeline Island in Lake Superior where my Ojibwe family originated long ago. . . . I pick mushrooms, explode puffballs, fall asleep next to my dog, and remember how difficult it was to remain quiet as a child.[5]

The reader is also given information about the little drawings throughout the book. Erdrich drew them from photographs of her children and her animals. She wrote,

> . . . my children have posed at various ages for photographs that I now keep catalogued in shoeboxes. The objects pictured are pieces from my own collection of traditionally made Ojibwe baskets and moccasins.[6]

The "Meet Louise Erdrich" page in the back of the book gives very personal details that a child as well as an adult fan would love to know. The interviewer writes that Erdrich and her family have "a very new dog, a very strange cat—both pitch black—and a garden devoted to rhubarb . . ." and that the stories of Omakayas were "inspired when Ms. Erdrich and her mother, Rita Gourneau Erdrich, were researching their own family history." This section goes on to state that "Ms. Erdrich is planning to write seven more books about Omakayas and her family, and the stories will span a hundred years of history."[7] Why seven more books? As mentioned earlier, Erdrich's children's series has been compared to the Laura Ingalls Wilder *Little House* books of which there are nine. If Erdrich does complete and publish seven more, the total number of her children's books would equal in number those of Wilder, and that may be her goal—to meet or exceed the number of books that Wilder wrote. In the interview section at the back of the book, Erdrich reveals that she has started the third book in the series, *Twelve Moons Running*. She offers nothing of the plot line, but ends the response to the question with, "I'd like to tell you more, but I have to write it first."[8]

Finally, the back pages of *The Game of Silence* include a photo of Erdrich with her dog, Cola. In Spanish, the word "cola" means tail, while in Lakota, a similar word means friend, and both are appropriate names for a beloved pet. The caption beneath the photo reads,

> Here I am with my old pal Cola, fiercely goofy, lovable, and also stubborn like me. I wanted my picture taken with him because he is seventeen and he is the inspiration for the dog in *The Game of Silence*.[9]

The photo is a head shot of Erdrich and Cola with Erdrich smiling pleasantly, the dog soulfully interested, both looking directly into the camera. In this one children's book, Erdrich reveals more of herself than she does in any three or four interviews, and a good deal more than she ever puts into her adult works, but that should not be surprising. She reveals what she wants known about herself at times and places of her own choosing. Like Fleur, she is a strong woman, but enigmatic, but that she should be most open with children is fitting. She is most open and frank when writing or talking about childbirth, raising children, and in conversations with children. Strangely, where many people are queasily uncomfortable talking about sex, and writers often find sex scenes difficult to write (how to make them seem real without descending into purple prose or making them so poetically obscure as to make the reader wonder if a sex act took place at all), Erdrich writes such scenes with grace and dignity and complete believability. There is no hesitation. In conversational interviews, Erdrich does not belabor the topic, but neither does she shy from it. Odd that the area most people would find uncomfortable does not seem to dismay her, but she is reluctant to reveal other mundane matters of her own life.

The sex scenes in her next novel, *The Painted Drum*, released in 2005, are classic Erdrich—frank and realistic, yet poetic and beautiful. The main character, Faye Travers, whose heritage is Euro-American and Ojibwe, like Erdrich, carries on an affair with a widowed sculptor who lives nearby. She is drawn to him as a person and for sex, of course, but she is riddled with guilt as well. She is afraid, it would seem, that she does not deserve to love and be loved because she believes she is responsible for her sister's death many years earlier. In this book, at least for some of the settings of the story, Erdrich draws upon her own experience of living both in New Hampshire and in the Ojibwe country of Minnesota and North Dakota. The title of the book comes from a drum that Faye, an estate sales agent, discovers among the possessions of a New Hampshire man who plundered native artifacts for his own personal interest. Faye steals the drum and returns it to the drum maker's descendants and in so doing rediscovers her own native heritage. As Erdrich is wont to do, there are two narrators here. One is Faye and the other is the descendant of the drum maker, Bernard Shaawano, who tells the story of how the drum came to be made.

Drums are an important aspect of Ojibwe cultural practice. Erdrich has grounded so many of her novels in the Ojibwe culture, it was probably inevitable that she would eventually incorporate the drum into the plot of one of her novels. She wrote about ceremonial belief and practice in connection with death often, as in the opening section of *Tracks*, and about the role of the mythological figure of the *windigo* in *Tracks* and *The Antelope Wife*, among other books. The power of the drum to revive and release destructive memory and to heal is at the center of the plot in *The Painted Drum*. The characters, though, are classic Erdrich. The main character of Faye is another strong woman, if not so self-confident and assured as Fleur or Margaret in *Tracks*. Some critics and readers think that Erdrich has not created equally strong and sympathetic men characters, and that view has some validity. Consider, for instance, the self-centered and needy Richard Whiteheart Beads in *The Antelope Wife*, the sneaky, underhanded behavior of Nector in *Tracks*, and the opportunistic, amoral Lyman Lammartine in *The Bingo Palace*. Asked about this seeming preference for strong female characters in an interview for the *Oakland Tribune*, Erdrich says that some [of the male characters] have not been "the most delightful" but that creating Bernard [Shawaano] for *The Painted Drum* was a different experience. "He is one of the wisest male characters I've ever written. I have a soft spot for the men in this book."[10]

Other readers might disagree about whether Bernard as the strongest male character, arguing instead that one of the strongest characters—male or female—that Erdrich ever created is that of Nanapush in *Tracks*, *Four Souls*, and other novels. He is a wise, grandfatherly figure, but tricksy and full of humor and human failings. Erdrich had strong male figures in her own life in the person of her brothers, her father Ralph, and her two grandfathers. On creating characters in general, she says,

> Sometimes I've no idea where their motivations and actions come from. I've no idea whether to attribute them to an unknown part of myself or something bigger outside myself, of if I'm like a wanderer in the woods, stumbling into their

world . . . They become part of my waking thoughts, and I return to them when I'm doing something else. But they don't take me over.[11]

This novel revisits familiar places in Ojibwe country from her other books as well as New Hampshire, which is a new setting for Erdrich's work. Of course, *The Painted Drum* is about relationships—that of Faye to her mother, from whom she seeks forgiveness over the death of her sister, and of Faye to her lover. National Public Radio interviewer Martha Woodruff remarked that it is difficult to think of "relationship" without thinking about the Erdrich–Dorris connection, a public closeness that Woodruff claims Erdrich says she "fostered in part to atone for her devotion to her art." Woodruff asked if Erdrich missed his [Dorris's] input in her writing life (his editing), and after a long silence, Erdrich responds with,

> Well, as a—you know, I said something about trying to get at the truth as a writer, and I'll try it as a person, too. No, I don't. And it kind of makes my heart jump a little to say that, but no, I don't miss it.[12]

After his death, Erdrich had been reluctant to speak out about the part of Dorris in her life, unwilling to raise those old ghosts, unwilling to open old wounds, unwilling to risk criticism from their mutual friends and acquaintances, and perhaps, in the Ojibwe way, unwilling to mention the name of the dead at all. Erdrich had finally come to a place where she could be honest. She had proven her ability to write without him, protected and nurtured their children, and gotten on with living. But she did not speak his name, or if she did, the interviewer did not record it.

There would be no new books—no poetry, no nonfiction, no novels—for more than two years, a negligible stretch of time for any other author, but an infinity for Erdrich. Such a lapse between publications had happened earlier in her career, from 1984–1986, and again from 1996–1998, but the 1984–1986 gap was when she had borne two daughters and was caring for her three adopted children as well as dealing with the egocentric behavior of Dorris. The second gap was during her separation from Dorris and his subsequent death. There seemed to be no major trauma or work-load issue for her in the period of 2005–2008. It was simply a time for rest and regrouping and for finishing the children's book, *The Game of Silence,* rather than writing the more work-intensive novels. She had been writing almost unremittingly for more than 20 years. Now, she was economically secure, her three eldest daughters were on their way to making lives of their own, and the youngest was in school and beyond needing constant attention and care. There is no public information about her relationship with Tobasonakwuk other than what Erdrich revealed in *Books and Islands,* but whatever happened for good or ill, she would keep it to herself after living her last marriage and its fatal ending under the microscope of public attention.

No doubt, she wrote, but most likely on several projects at once, so that no one of them came to fruition quickly. However, two projects did reach publication in 2008: another novel, *The Plague of Doves,* and another children's book, *The Porcupine Year.*

For *The Plague of Doves,* Erdrich followed her long-established practice of taking previously written short stories, writing new short stories, and then weaving them in their entirety or in bits into a novel. One original story for this novel, "Satan: Highjacker of a Planet," dates back 10 years to its first publication in *The Atlantic Monthly,* and was reprinted in *Prize Stories 1998.* Other parts of the novel appeared as short stories from 2005–2007 in *The New Yorker, The Atlantic Monthly,* and *North Dakota Quarterly* and were reprinted in *The O.Henry Prize Stories,* and in yearly editions of *The Best American Short Stories* and *The Best American Mystery Stories.*

The Plague of Doves has no dedication page. After publishing and writing dedications for 21 books of creative nonfiction, poetry, and novels, it would seem she has honored almost everyone. On an unlabeled page at the end of the book, however, she does issue "thank yous" to her editors and four other people whose identities beyond the names are not disclosed.

Erdrich's fertile imagination takes wing within the plot of this book—her eye for the quirkiness of human behavior as well as the mundane and her penchant for extrapolating upon Ojibwe history and culture. The story is based upon a real event: the hanging of a 13-year-old boy, Paul Holy Track, by a mob in Emmons County, North Dakota. Another historical character in the book, Louis Riel, was a Métis resistance leader against the Canadian government in the late 19th century. The other characters are uniquely Erdrich, but familiar to her readers, if not as the same characters from her previous novels, but as representative of the kinds of people she imagines into life.

The book garnered her the usual starred reviews[13] from *Publishers Weekly* and *Booklist.* A newspaper from her old haunt in New Hampshire, the *Concord Monitor* included this in its review of the book,

> The *Plague of Doves,* her 11th novel, is yet another of her superb enchantments . . . Since the publication of her first book, *Love Medicine,* and her subsequent sagas of Plains people, Erdrich has demonstrated a rare ability to create vibrant, wholly original characters and to describe nature in prose so lyrical it becomes poetry. *The Plague of Doves* is proof that she has yet to exhaust her powerful magic.[14]

Almost, but not quite magic, the book was a finalist for the greatest prize in American letters—The Pulitzer, but was not the winner.

Nor had she exhausted her powerful magic in the realm of children's literature, either. *The Porcupine Year,* the third book in the Omakayas series, came out in 2008 and earned starred reviews from *Kirkus, Kliatt, School Library Journal,* and *Booklist.* The previous book in this series, *The Game of Silence,* won the prestigious Scott O'Dell Award for Historical Fiction, which probably generated interest for this new one.[15]

This book, like *The Plague of Doves*, does not have a dedication page, and most of the end material is repeated from information published in *The Game of Silence*, although the specific information for creating a family tree has been shortened into a narrative without the accompanying graphic illustrations. Some information has been added to the end material, specifically a paragraph on storytelling and another on "cool crafts," but the latter is just a list without specific how-to details. This book, too, is illustrated with drawings in Erdrich's style, although there is no information as to whether she actually drew these herself or whether someone else created them. The third in the series of nine that she has set for herself, *Chickadee*, was published in August 2012. This book continues the saga of Omakayas through the perspective of her sons. The book that most clearly defines Erdrich's talent and her writing style would not be published until 2009. *The Red Convertible* contains almost 500 pages of her short stories, 36 stories to be exact, of which 26 were previously published and 10 were new. Reading through this book is like visiting all the days of her life from childhood to middle age, like seeing all the seeds that were valuable in their own right as tiny perfect bits of nature, and recognizing in these stories the seeds that grew into the mighty trees of the novels. Here are all the characters that populate her work, the settings in Ojibwe country, the mythology, the comedy, and the pathos. A review of the book for the *Minneapolis Tribune* states,

> Nearly every novel Louise Erdrich has published began life as a short story. "I am certain that I have come to the end," she explains in the preface to "The Red Convertible," her collection of fabulously sexy and selected tales. "But the stories are rarely finished with me. They gather force and weight and complexity," and then—presumably—they take flight.[16]

There are more starred reviews, including one from *Publishers Weekly;* all are unanimous in praising this book as well as the body of Erdrich's work. Some critics consider this an introduction to her work for those who have never read her before, and most of them recommend the book as a reminder of the great novels she produced using these stories as take-off points. However, for some readers, this book might be the Cliff's Notes on Erdrich, and after having read this, they might see no point in reading her extended repertoire. Most of the reviewer's compliments are reserved for the previously published stories, not the newer ones, and one reviewer takes aim at the newest stories as not being up to the usual Erdrich quality. Charles May wrote,

> The more recent stories are somewhat less compelling . . . and when she leaves her mysterious American Indians . . . Erdrich, from whom we have come to expect the extraordinary, just seems ordinary. . . . Still this is a book worth reading, if for no other reason than to have some of the best parts of Erdrich's earlier work gathered together in one place.[17]

Although the reviewers do not say so exactly, it would seem that many of them view this work as Erdrich's Greatest Hits, which is not a negative reaction. Greatest Hits CDs for musicians often sell far more copies than their other CDs that might have had one to three good songs on each. From a commercial point of view, *The Red Convertible* was certainly successful.

Such a collection, whether selected works of a writer or the songs of a musician, is often viewed as the summing-up of a career and an assumption that the career is on the back end and winding down. For Erdrich, perhaps the trajectory has not yet reached the high point.

NOTES

1. Louise Erdrich, *Four Souls* (New York: HarperCollins, 2004).

2. Andrew Wiley, Agent, *Publishers Weekly,* July 2, 2004.

3. Carole Goldberg, "From Louise Erdrich's Great Plains, a tale of revenge," *Hartford Courant,* July 7, 2004.

4. Louise Erdrich, *The Game of Silence* (New York: HarperTrophy, an imprint of HarperCollins, 2005), 15.

5. Erdrich, *The Game of Silence,* 3.

6. Ibid.

7. Ibid., 5.

8. Ibid., 7.

9. Photo by Anne Marsden, *The Game of Silence,* 4.

10. Diane Weddington, "Author Louise Erdrich says creating characters can be painful," *Oakland Tribune,* October 4, 2005.

11. Ibid.

12. Martha Woodruff, "Profile: Louise Erdrich and the 'Painted Drum,'" *National Public Radio,* NPR Weekend Edition, October 2, 2005.

13. Publications that review books as their main thrust of their periodicals, such as *Publishers Weekly* and *Booklist,* offer the "starred review" to books that they deem particularly outstanding. Most of Erdrich's books have earned these honors, even those that have been criticized by the same publication that issued the starred review. It would seem that starring any book she publishes has become almost automatic.

14. Carole Goldberg, "Another enchantment from Louise Erdrich: Powerful novels[sic] spans 100 years on Plains," *Concord Monitor,* May 11, 2008.

15. The Scott O'Dell Award was established in 1982. It awards $5,000 for a meritorious book published in the previous year for a children or young adults.

16. John Freeman, "Raw Power; Short Stories: Thirty years of short fiction by Minnesota author Louise Erdrich show her to be a master of the form (VARIETY)," *Minneapolis Star Tribune,* January 11, 2009.

17. Charles E. May, Book Review: *The Red Convertible. Milwaukee Journal-Sentinel,* January 3, 2009.

EIGHT

From Page to Stage and Beyond

A new novel and a stage version of Erdrich's previously published *The Master Butcher's Singing Club* were Erdrich's literary contributions to 2010. The attempt at translating Erdrich's works from the page to the stage began when director Francesca Zambello came to Minneapolis in the summer of 2009 to direct her stage version of Laura Ingalls Wilder's *Little House on the Prairie,* and spent much time at the Kenwood Café next door to the Erdrich sisters's Birchbark Book Store. Zambello came into the bookstore from time to time, where she picked up a copy of *The Master Butcher's Singing Club.* That fateful encounter led Zambello to approach Erdrich about staging the novel as a play, bringing in Pulitzer Prize-winning playwright Marsha Norman to condense the book into a stage version. It was odd that Erdrich, who wrote the anti-Little House children's book series, would become invested in a project created by the woman who produced a musical based on one of the Ingalls-Wilder novels. Erdrich stated, "Ma [a character in the Little House series] was a racist, and there's no way around it." Little House never gets around to suggesting what it was like for native people to be "invaded by Pa and his ax."[1]

The Marsha Norman adaptation of Erdrich's novel played at the Guthrie Theater in Minneapolis from September 9, 2010, to October 30. The reviews were not, of course, about the book version of the story, but about the stage version, the acting, the set design, and all that goes into making a play, rather than the considerations of what goes into writing a novel. Erdrich advised on the project, but did not take an active role in translating the work from novel to play. The reviews were mixed, as in this one, where the reviewer compliments the cast members' acting ability (particularly Lee Mark Nelson as the butcher), offers a summary of the plot, and compliments Erdrich's original novel, but went on to say,

> . . . The difficulty of editing an epic down to size becomes apparent . . . the story suffers from its faithfulness to the script . . . A couple of historical characters step in, as though at Ft. Snelling, to dramatize the retelling. It feels false at best.[2]

Another review in *Variety* was kinder, if measured in the response to the play,

> This elegant adaptation by Marsha Norman . . . of a sweeping multi-decade novel, "The Master Butcher's Singing Club," puts forth impressive contributions all around. Norman's script captures the essential delicate nature of Midwestern author Louise Erdrich's prose, and spreads just enough narration among characters to keep things moving without making it feel like you're being read to.[3]

In a *Theater Journal* review of the play from September 25, 2010, Robert Hubbard also gave a mixed report,

> The Guthrie deserves credit for undertaking ambitious productions like *The Master Butcher's Singing Club* . . . several creative and sensitive attempts to highlight clashing cultures within the story served the production well; flourishes of fine acting, lovely imagery, and inventive design produced many delightful moments. If only the promise of the production could have overcome an unfortunate misfire in the depiction of Cyprian [a gay character within the story], as well as a wandering and unfocused script.[4]

Not one of the reviewers criticized Erdrich, nor should they have. A writer's work stands on its own; what readers or other artists do with that work after publication is usually not under the control of the original author. Marsha Norman is a prize-winning playwright, but this is simply not her best work. Scheduled to run through October 30, the play closed five days early.

Reviewer Marianne Combs blamed not the quality of the production but rather the management of the Guthrie Theater. A representative of the theater stated that the play was closing early because tickets were not selling. Combs argued that the reason the tickets were not selling was not because the play was of poor quality (she also gave it a mixed review), but because the Guthrie had scheduled *The Master Butcher's Singing Club* opposite a proven production. She states,

> *The Great Game: Afghanistan* ran from September 29–October 17, creating serious competition for Guthrie audiences for a large chunk of TMBSC's run. *The Great Game: Afghanistan* came with rave reviews in hand, while TMBSC was a world premiere, with no stage pedigree.[5]

Thus, the translation of Erdrich's work from novel to stage was short lived, with only one small after note—The Southhampton Writers Conference at Stony Brook, NY, for the summer of 2011 chose Marsha Norman as a workshop leader in playwriting for the event, and on July 17, Norman offered a reading of the play in the Avram Theater in association with the resident theater company at the Writers Conference, New York's Ensemble Studio Theatre.[6] The play was only marginally successful, but Erdrich had another, different success earlier in the year to look back upon with pleasure.

In January of 2010, her 13th novel (not counting *The Crown of Columbus*) was released and caused a great flurry of interest, but not necessarily for the usual reasons. *Shadow Tag* details a failing marriage with a wife falling into alcoholism, confused and traumatized children, and a husband who is a manipulative and egocentric artist. The husband in the story, Gil, is an artist who has built his career from a single subject—multiple paintings of his wife, Irene, but these are no ordinary portraits. Gil paints her naked in sexually suggestive poses that border on soft porn. He is a parasite at worst, and at best, a deluded man who uses his wife's beauty to further his own career. He does not truly love her, but needs her, objectifies, and uses her. Eventually, Irene can no longer tolerate his demanding, manipulative behavior. Nevertheless, she cannot bring herself to confront him directly. Instead, *she* manipulates him. A writer of journals, she knows that he reads what she writes in them, so she deliberately plants misinformation—that she is having affairs—in the Red Journal, while keeping a second one, the Blue Notebook, in a safe deposit vault where her true thoughts and actions are recorded. Gil is not only destroying their marriage, he is also physically abusing their children.

Although this novel is a thinly disguised biography of the Erdrich–Dorris relationship, most reviewers completely ignored that fact, as if it were not an elephant in the room. One reviewer who did address the issue straight on was Ron Charles, writing for *The Washington Post,* who stated the obvious—that readers would certainly recognize the characters and plot as originating directly from Erdrich's personal experience, which Charles labels as "voyeuristic temptations." He then praises Erdrich for drawing on her own experience to create a work of fiction that he believes is about universal tragedy, not simply Erdrich's private experiences.[7]

Oddly, though, Charles writes that modern writers cannot or will not transform personal trauma into universal experience—odd, because it would seem that it is recognition of the universal in personal tragedy or triumph that keeps posters and lurkers on social media sites returning again and again to the stories they read there. Admittedly those who post stories of personal experience on social media sites are not professional writers, not usually anyway, but rather everyday people. Still, Charles offers no evidence to support his assertion.

Overall, however, Charles's review is probably the most balanced of all the reviews printed. He recognizes, where many other reviewers do not, that the style in this novel is different from her earlier novels, stating, ". . . she keeps

'Shadow Tag' tightly focused, abandoning entirely the discursive style of her previous books." He continued with, "What would have been oppressively grim in a longer work remains arresting in this taut tale, which comes to us from the three narrators as a series of finely cut moments, each just a page or two long."[8]

Another reviewer who took on the obvious is Patrick Condon, who wrote,

> Readers familiar with Erdrich's life story will certainly see echoes in "Shadow Tag." In 1997, her estranged husband, the writer Michael Dorris, committed suicide amid allegations of child abuse—events that parallel some of the plot strands in "Shadow Tag." But knowledge of that history isn't necessary to admire Erdrich's accomplishments here, as she weaves painfully realistic depictions of alcoholism and abuse into a domestic drama that builds an almost thrillerlike momentum.[9]

Another reviewer, who like Ron Charles, not only addressed the commonalities between this novel and Erdrich's private life, but also the issues of the very different writing style is Leah Hager Cohen:

> . . . in places, "Shadow Tag" seems more like notes for a novel than fully realized fiction. ("The tragic irony of it offended him." "His outlook was sentimental while hers was tragic." "They might hate each other, at least, Irene might hate Gil, while he had no idea how much he hated Irene because he was so focused on winning back her love.") Elsewhere though, Erdrich's unbridled urgency yields startlingly original phrasing ("the christbirthing pinecone air") as well as flashes of blinding lucidity.[10]

Here, Cohen recognizes the novel's different style, and demonstrates those differences with examples from *Shadow Tag*. Erdrich's style, though different from what she usually employs, is not "wrong" or "bad" or even, as Cohen suggests merely "notes for a novel." Ernest Hemingway, for instance, used short declarative sentences, but no one has ever said that *The Sun Also Rises* (or any of his other novels) is merely notes for a novel. It is tempting to do so with Erdrich, however, because her other works are written in a style more reminiscent of William Faulkner than Hemingway. Like Faulkner, Erdrich wrote beautifully poetic and descriptive long flowing sentences. *Shadow Tag* partakes more of Hemingway than Faulkner. However, Cohen gets it exactly right when she discusses the problem of whether to compare the novel with Erdrich's own life:

> It's a fool's errand to parse fact from fiction. Even given such glaring similarities, to acknowledge them in a review would seem prurient, loathsome—if Erdrich hadn't seeded her narrative with what feels like an imperative to do so.[11]

She has put her finger on the reason why so many reviewers of this novel chose to ignore the obvious connections between fact and fiction—"to review them would seem prurient, loathsome." She is also exactly right when she states that Erdrich, purposely or not, invites such comparisons, tantalizes knowledgeable readers to wonder whether she did or did not drink heavily during the last years of her marriage, whether or not Dorris did invade Erdrich's privacy by reading her journals, and so on. And yet, in making such comparisons, even wondering about them, many readers, including this author, felt fascinated and yet horrified by their own fascination, as if they had dreamed of being a window peeper, woke up and found themselves standing outside a window, observing a sexual act between strangers taking place beyond the pane.

It seems odd that Erdrich would choose to play out in public what she had declared in so many interviews as being a topic she did not wish to discuss, even though she became more forthright as the years passed. Recall that at one point she told an interviewer that she did not believe in "trying a man in the press after he is dead and judging him guilty or innocent."[12] This is the sturdily spoken belief that most people have been taught from childhood, that it is wrong to speak ill of the dead because they are not there to offer a defense. Still, if a person made errors, minor or major, while they were alive, dying does not negate those errors, nor should it bestow a halo where none was deserved.

Of course, part of Erdrich's reluctance to discuss Dorris's private failings and personal anguish may have been because few, if any, of their friends and acquaintances were aware of those problems and most openly declared their puzzlement and confusion when Dorris committed suicide. If Erdrich had spoken at length of Dorris's failings back when Dorris first died, she might have been accused of lying at worst and at best of breaking the commonly held social pact that one should not speak ill of the dead. Dorris left her without a defense, manipulating her even after his death.

Viewed in that light, *Shadow Tag* is not Erdrich working out her psychological trauma in public, nor is it an attempt to malign a dead person. Rather, it is Erdrich's courageous attempt to defend herself in the best way she knows how: through writing fiction. If some of her readers are embarrassed or confused by this effort, then that is something over which she has no control. She has had her say and that will probably be the end of that discussion. Occasional themes of suicide, of marital strife, of child abuse, or other personally lived trauma may still appear in her future work, but that is what a writer does—takes their own experience and their own observations of the experience of others and weaves tales that astonish or shock or delight—sometimes all three. We only read of it, but the author has to live with it.

What the readers of this new novel did not know, nor did the people who attended the theater production of *The Master Butcher's Singing Club* in the summer of 2010, was that Erdrich was enduring a private health crisis at the same time. She had been diagnosed with early stage breast cancer and was undergoing aggressive treatment, which made her hair fall out, at the very moment the play opened. She stated that she had sat in the audience wearing a "gorgeous wig," terrified that a fate that had befallen one of the characters in *The Master Butcher* might also be her own fate.[13] Demonstrating strength and tenacity that she has always owned while others in similar situations have succumbed to despair, Erdrich is now free of cancer, and two years later, in the fall of 2012, has two new books out. Perhaps, that is where the strength to face life's most difficult challenges lies: in her writing, but also in her family. Those two seem to be the wells from which she draws the healing power to survive all. In the afterword to this latest novel, *The Round House,* Erdrich thanks members of her family for their support during this difficult time, but she specifically thanks her daughters, Persia, Pallas, Aza, and Nenaa'ikiizhikok.

The Round House addresses the issue of violence against women of color, and against Native American women in particular, which, coincidentally, was the subject of this author's first novel, *Elsie's Business.*[14] In Erdrich's novel, just turned 13-year-old Joe Coutts narrates the story, one of the only instances where Erdrich does not employ multiple narrators to tell the story. Joe is the only child of the May/December marriage of Geraldine and Bazil Coutts. The pregnancy was such a surprise that Joe is given the nickname "Oops," perhaps something that Erdrich herself felt when she found herself in her early forties and pregnant for the fourth time with daughter Nenaa'kiizhikok.

Young Joe says, "I'd always had the perfect family—loving, rich by reservation standards, stable—the family you would never run away from. No more."[15] The situation that young Joe wants to escape is the rape of his mother, Geraldine, which is horrific enough, but Geraldine's withdrawal into passivity and mental instability is perhaps as horrific as the event itself. Some reviewers have called this novel a coming-of-age story, and that it is, but in most coming-of-age stories, the event that propels the young person from child to adult is something often so innocuous that adults within the story are unaware of it. Here, Joe is not nudged gently into adulthood, but thrust, as violently and rudely as the crime of rape itself. His early reaction to what happened is understandable, perhaps predictable when he says, "I wanted to know that whoever had attacked my mother would be found, punished and killed."[16]

While the story told here may be Erdrich's best ever written, a story that can be appreciated for the beautiful way it is crafted, this is also a book about social justice for which the story is the carrier. Erdrich draws upon multiple areas wherein American Indians still face challenges in obtaining justice, such as the Major Crimes Act of 1885, which places jurisdiction over seven major crime categories committed on Indian reservations under the FBI, regardless of whether the perpetrator of the crime is an American Indian or not. In other words, for any major crime committed *on an Indian reservation,* the tribal police do not have the authority to investigate or prosecute, but must call in the FBI, and therein lies multiple problems. First, in any criminal investigation near a reservation, someone must determine exactly where the crime was committed to determine who has jurisdiction, and this quibbling and dallying can and often does delay investigations, allow time for crime scenes to be degraded or disturbed, and ultimately delay or deny justice for the victim. In *The Round House,* Erdrich explores the problems of jurisdiction in the investigation of

Geraldine's rape. The fogginess, in some cases, rigidity of federal, state, and local laws and policies in relation to American Indians makes it more difficult to solve crimes committed against them. The instances of rape among American Indian women is one of the most shocking of all crimes committed against American Indian people in general. In the Afterword of *The Round House,* Erdrich wrote:

> This book is set in 1988, but the tangle of laws that hinder prosecution of rape cases on many reservations still exists. "Maze of Justice," a 2009 report by Amnesty International included the following statistics: 1 in 3 Native women will be raped in her lifetime (and that figure is certainly higher as Native women often do not report rape); 86 per cent of rapes and sexual assaults upon Native women are perpetrated by non-Native men; few are prosecuted.[17]

No reader should be surprised that Erdrich is referencing historical instances of injustice, although perhaps, with the exception of *A Plague of Doves,* she has usually not included references to specific laws and policies that affect Native Americans. Her writing here is a return to that lyrical style she has more commonly used than the cryptic, shorthand style of her previous novel, *Shadow Tag.* In *The Round House,* she also uses that time slippage in the narrative that is typical of her work. For example, early in the novel, Joe as a 13-year-old narrator slips into the future Joe that he will be as an adult. Erdrich writes, in Joe's perspective, "Much later after I had gone into law and gone back and examined every document I could find . . . "

The reviews that are available (as of this writing in early 2013), are uniformly complimentary, with never a naysayer anywhere. For example, Michiko Kakutani of the *New York Times,* who has reviewed multiple Erdrich novels, wrote that *The Round House* is a powerful novel, worth reading,[18] while the *Minneapolis Star Tribune* called the book an "artfully balanced mystery."[19] *Publishers Weekly* gave the novel a coveted starred review, stating that "The story pulses with urgency as [Erdrich] probes the moral and legal ramifications of a terrible act of violence."[20]

In March 2013, Congress passed and President Barack Obama signed the Violence Against Women Act, a renewal of a previous law with some additions, which among other provisions remedies the exact issue that Erdrich addressed in *The Round House.* Prior to the passage of this act, White men who abused American Indian women on reservations could not be prosecuted by the tribal court system, which meant that White men usually escaped justice for these crimes. Perhaps, Erdrich's book played some role in righting this injustice.

In November 2012, *The Round House* won the prestigious National Book Award. There were four other contenders for this annual award including Junot Diaz for *This Is How You Lose Her,*[21] but Erdrich was the only woman nominated for this year's award. Diaz, like Erdrich is also a recipient of the Guggenheim Fellowship, often called the genius award. Erdrich is the only woman writer nominated.

The second book, *Chickadee,* that Erdrich published in 2012 is the fourth children's book in her Birchbark series.[22] As previously stated, this one takes up the next generation of the Omakayas character Erdrich first created in the Birchbark series. The plot features two brothers, Chickadee and Makoons, who become separated early in the story. Chickadee then goes on a quest to reunite with his brother, counting on the strength of his namesake chickadee to help him. In the back pages included in Erdrich's third book in the series, *The Game of Silence,* Erdrich stated that she had started the fourth book in the series, which she titled *Twelve Moons Running.* Something changed, obviously. Perhaps that book morphed into *Chickadee,* or perhaps *Twelve Moons Running* is yet a different book that will come out at some time in the future.

Interestingly, other reviewers of this children's book series are also comparing them to the Laura Ingalls Wilder Little House series. A reviewer for the *New York Times* wrote:

> [In this] story of a young Ojibwa girl, Omakayas, living on an island in Lake Superior around 1847, Louise Erdrich is reversing the narrative perspective used in most children's stories about nineteenth-century Native Americans. Instead of looking out at 'them' as dangers or curiosities, Erdrich, drawing on her family's history, wants to tell about 'us', from the inside. The Birchbark House establishes its own ground, in the vicinity of Laura Ingalls Wilder's 'Little House' books.[23]

To equal Wilder's seven books in the Little House series, Erdrich needs to publish only three more, but it would not be surprising for Erdrich, perhaps one of the most prolific modern authors in any genre, to far exceed that number.

NOTES

1. Michael Tortorello, "Staging Erdrich," *Minnesota Monthly,* September 1, 2010.

2. Tom Gihring, "Review: Guthrie's "Master Butcher's Singing Club" Hits Mostly High Notes," *Minnesota Monthly,* October 2010.

3. Review, The Master Butcher's Singing Club, *Variety,* http:www.variety.com/review/VE117943656/.

4. Robert Hubbard, Review: *The Master Butcher's Singing Club. Theater Journal,* September 25, 2010, *Project Muse,* http://muse.jhu.edu.

5. Marianne Combs, "Why is the Master Butcher's Singing Club closing early?" *MPR News,* October 26, 2010.

6. Southampton Writers Conference Press Release, http:www.stonybrook.edu/writers/writers/reservations.shtml

7. Ron Charles, "Love in the time of bitterness," *The Washington Post,* February 3, 2010.

8. Ibid.

9. Patrick Condon, "Compelling 'Shadow Tag' a departure for Erdrich," *AP Worldstream,* February 12, 2010.

10. Leah Hager Cohen, "Cruel Love," *The New York Times Sunday Book Review,* February 5, 2010.

11. Ibid.

12. Staff writer, "Wife Claims Dorris Was Suicidal For Years: Only She Knew of His Tormented Secret," *Seattle Post-Intelligencer,* April 19, 1997.

13. Rohan Preston, "With New Novel Out, Erdrich Is Exulting in Life," *Minneapolis Star Tribune,* September 30, 2012.

14. Frances Washburn, *Elsie's Business* (Lincoln: University of Nebraska Press, 2006).

15. Louise Erdrich, *The Round House* (New York: Harper, 2012), 96.

16. Ibid., 12.

17. Ibid., Afterword.

18. Michiko Kakutani, "Ambushed on the Road to Manhood: 'The Round House,' Louise Erdrich's New Novel," *New York Times,* October 15, 2012.

19. James Cihlar, "Fiction: *The Round House,*" by Louise Erdrich, *Minneapolis Star Tribune,* September 29, 2012.

20. *Publishers Weekly,* July 16, 2012.

21. Junot Diaz, *This Is How You Lose Her* (New York: Riverhead Press, 2012).

22. Louise Erdrich, *Chickadee* (New York: HarperCollins, 2012).

23. *New York Times,* Quoted on Barnes & Noble webpage, http://www.Barnesand noble.com/w/birchbark-house-louise-erdrich/1100541474.

NINE

A Place at the Table

That Louise Erdrich has earned and deserves a place in the canon of writers is undisputed, although scholars may argue over who else should sit at the table and whether Erdrich should sit at the head of that group, or to one side, or at a roundtable of equals. Erdrich's work can be comfortably juxtaposed with writers of many different identities. The broadest category could be simply women writers and men writers; then, people of color in general, a category that could be subdivided into world writers and American writers. A further subdivision of the American category would include African American, Latino/a, Asian American, and American Indian. Erdrich had predecessors, both male and female writers in multiple categories, who opened a way for her to follow. She has stood upon the shoulders of giants.

Until quite recently in historical times, the word "woman" was not an adjective that could be applied to the noun "writer." As Olwen Hufton detailed in her book, *The Prospect Before Her: A History of Women in Western Europe, 1500–1800*,[1] women had two main career choices—marriage or the convent. Of course, there were women who made other choices, but these brave or unfortunate souls, depending upon the point of view, were often outcasts of society—spinsters, prostitutes, witches, or only an unwanted female relative that a family might grudgingly support as a member of the household, often in a servile position. Women who married faced the distinct possibility of early death from complications of childbirth in a time when antibiotics or even casual hygiene was unknown. Women who did survive were rarely educated, but spent most of their time caring for their children and households and often helping their spouses in the fields or in small shops to produce food and income.

Entering a convent was not a possible choice for many women because, first of all, she had to have the permission of a male relative, usually her father, but possibly a brother or even an uncle. Then, many convents expected that their postulants would bring a certain sum of money with them, comparable to a dowry. A woman without a dowry could neither marry nor enter a convent. Such women became the spinsters who lived with other family members in exchange for their work, whether domestic, agricultural, or crafts. The only avenue, with rare exceptions however, for a woman who wished to become literate or even aspire to writing herself, was to enter a convent. Until at least the 15th century, religious orders, primarily monasteries, were the repositories of learning and books, which not only created books but maintained libraries of books and educated some children of the wealthy, but only male children, of course. That situation began to change in the 16th century. Hufton writes, "Between 1500 and 1800 the number of women who seized the pen and of those who went further and inched into print multiplied very considerably."[2] Not surprisingly, some of the first women writers were nuns such as Saint Teresa of Avila, Angelica Baitelli, and Arcangela Tarbotta who all wrote religious tracts and letters and lives of the saints, particularly women saints.[3] By the 16th century, some women, particularly those who came from wealthy families with liberal fathers, were literate, but not necessarily writers. Women who did write expanded their repertoire from religious topics to works that offered advice on household management or child care. Their work, however, was usually edited by their religious confessor. One woman who stepped outside the boundaries of propriety and custom was the playwright Aphra Behn, "who carries the distinction of probably being the first woman to make a living from her literary oeuvre."[4] Her acquaintance with nobility and commoners alike provided her with ample material for her plays, of which 16 were published. A bold woman of dubious reputation, she defended a woman's right to study science and philosophy, but she wrote sexually explicit material that Erdrich has probably read and appreciated for their frank and open descriptions of sexual play.

Meanwhile, in the new world of America, a few women wrote and published, but mostly on religious subjects such as the already discussed captivity narrative of Mary Rowlandson, although, there is now some doubt as to whether Rowlandson actually wrote her own story or whether it might have been ghost written by Cotton Mather.[5] Another early American woman writer, Anne Bradstreet (1612–1672) as the privileged daughter of an upper class country estate manager, Thomas Dudley, was better educated than most young women of her time. In her youth, she wrote poems to please her father, and she continued writing after her marriage. Always in ill health, she probably wrote most during the times she was bedridden. Her brother-in-law, John Woodbridge, took a manuscript of her poetry to London and had it printed there in 1650. No Aphra Behn, Bradstreet's poems reflect her concern for family and everyday life, along with some more contemplative philosophical works.[6]

In the early 18th century, Elizabeth Ashbridge published in the then popular genre of religious conversation. Born in England, at age 14, she ran away with a man who died shortly thereafter, and unwanted back at home, she emigrated first to Ireland, and then to America. Eventually she experienced a religious epiphany, became a Quaker, and wrote about that conversion as well as life for women in England and American during that time period.[7]

Nineteenth-century French writer, Amantine Lucile Aurore Dupin, illustrates the difficulties of getting published for a woman writer. Taking the pen name of George Sand, she wrote novels, literary criticism, and political texts in the mid-1800s. Contemporaries of Sand, the Bronte sisters of England were also successful novelists whose works are still read and respected. Charlotte, perhaps the most famous, wrote *Jane Eyre,* under the pen name of Currer Bell. Emily, author of *Wuthering Heights,* also wrote in the same romantic style as Charlotte, but the younger sister Anne used a more realistic style for her best known work, *The Tenant of Wildfell Hall.*

Some 50 years before George Sand and the Bronte sisters, a very few African Americans had begun to write for publication. Olaudah Equiano did not, however, define himself as African American nor Anglo-African but rather as "the African." Born in Nigeria, he was transported first to Barbados, and later to America, where he saw the worst of life as a slave. Purchased by a Quaker, Robert King, Equiano eventually bought his freedom and made his living as a servant and musician. His autobiography, *The Interesting Narrative of the Life of Olaudah Equiano, or Gustavus Vassa, the African,* was published in London in 1789, reprinted in New York in 1791. Less than 50 years later, another man of African descent, Frederick Douglass, would publish *Narrative of the Life of Frederick Douglass,* a written record of his life as a slave that he had been describing for years in public lectures. Concerned not only with oppression of people of color, Douglass was an active proponent of women's suffrage, and was an important influence on future black leaders.

Between Equiano and Douglass, another American man of color published his own autobiography. William Apess, a Native American of the Pequot tribe who in 1829 published *A Son of the Forest: The Experience of William Appes, A Native of the Forest, Comprising a Notice of the Pequod Tribe of Indians, Written by Himself.* Written as a Christian conversion narrative, Appes used the format to comment upon injustices perpetrated upon American Indians.

The 19th and early 20th centuries saw more American women writers published—Harriet Beecher Stowe, Emily Dickinson, Kate Chopin, Charlotte Perkins Gilman, and Edith Wharton, and a few African Americans including Booker T. Washington and W. E. B. Dubois, among others. The first Native American woman writer was not a U.S. citizen, however, but a Canadian.

Indigenous people have been in the Americas for hundreds of thousands of years without acknowledging human-created invisible lines on the land that divide counties, countries, states, or nations. Writing, too, is confined only by human-created boundaries. While many people think of American Indians as only those native people within the United States, in fact, Indigenous people have lived, worked, and yes, written throughout the entire archipelago of the western hemisphere. Native people referred to the U.S.–Canadian border as the "medicine line," indicating that it is a magic line on the ground, something that has significance, but does not exist in the real world. E. Pauline Johnson, born in 1861 of the Mohawk Nation in Canada, was the first American Indian woman writer who achieved publication and some degree of public attention.

Beginning publication in 1886, she wrote poetry and short fiction for children, but garnered most attention for her public performances, where she wore traditional clothing for the first half of her presentation, then changed and wore mainstream Victorian attire for the second half. Some critics called her work derivative and shallow and said that her public appearances were mere showmanship, but whether her writing was "good" or her method of delivering that work was useful is not the point. She was a native woman writer, the first to boldly declare that combination of ethnicity and literary ambition, unafraid of criticism.

The first American Indian writer south of the medicine line was Zitkala Sa (Gertrude Bonnin Simmons), and like Erdrich many years later, Zitkala Sa also came from the Upper Great Plains. She was Dakota, born on the Yankton Reservation. Like Erdrich, Zitkala Sa, left home to earn an education. As an elementary school student in the late 19th century, she attended an eastern boarding school. The experience was far from what Zitkala Sa expected. The boarding school experience, as for most American Indian children, was abusive and traumatic, but Zitkala Sa was determined to prove that her scholarship and intellect were as good as that of a White person. She persevered, particularly with writing and publishing, where she was determined to demonstrate American Indian literary and intellectual ability. She wrote a mix of political pieces, autobiographical essays, and short stories that were published from 1900–1904, then again from 1916–1924. Just as Erdrich's short stories were well received and published in *The Atlantic Monthly,* so were many of Zitkala Sa's early writings. A feisty woman, she refused to be denigrated as an Indian person, as a woman, or as a writer, but spoke and wrote with skill, honesty, and superior intellectual ability.[8]

Other than their geographical origins and native ancestry, there is little in common between Zitkala Sa and Erdrich. Zitkala Sa was a writer, yes, but better known for her political activism and social commentary than for her literary writing. Further, Zitkala Sa was neither a novelist nor poet, but a writer of short pieces that were mostly autobiographical or political in style and theme. Without Zitkala Sa, Erdrich would certainly have still became a writer, but both E. Pauline Johnson and Zitkala Sa provided the early impetus for all American Indian women who aspired to step outside the accepted roles of women in general and American Indian women in particular.

The first Native American woman novelist from the United States was Mourning Dove (Christine Quintasket) from the Colville Confederated Tribes of eastern Washington state. Born in 1885, her parents were poor and uneducated but respected within their tribal society. Realizing that education was a key to achieving any success in the world, Mourning Dove sought her own education, first at the Goodwin Catholic Mission School, then at Colville Mission, Fort Spokane, Fort Shaw, and eventually at Calgary College, but her total years of education from all these institutions were only nine. Later, she would enroll in a business school to improve her typing and writing skills. She married early and often, mostly to men who were abusive or, at best, only tolerant of her ambitions to be a writer.

She began writing a novel in 1912 as a reaction to a western romance novel set among the Flathead Indians that she felt was unsympathetic towards the Indian characters. Deciding that her own work was flawed, probably in the basic writing and grammar, she hid it away. Soon afterwards, she sought more education at a Calgary business school. A chance encounter at the Walla Walla Frontier Days celebration brought her into contact with Lucullus Virgil McWhorter, a Yakima businessman and Indian rights advocate. McWhorter urged her to preserve her Salish traditions through writing, and it was this contact that led him to become her editor for her novel, *Cogewea, the Half-Blood*.[9]

The book is at its heart the romance novel that Mourning Dove intended, but McWhorter's heavy handed, preachy additions to Mourning Dove's text make for tedious reading. Long sections added by McWhorter, while well-intentioned, belabor the injustice of society and Federal Indian law and policies in regard to America's Indigenous population, bogging down the plot to a point where it is almost unreadable. An expurgated version more faithful to Mourning Dove's original work and intent would be of great service to the genre of American Indian literature and to Mourning Dove herself.

Besides the series of difficult and tempestuous marriages, Mourning Dove was often in poor health and always struggling financially. She worked for a while as a teacher, probably the highest paying and most personally satisfying job she ever held, but mostly her life was a series of temporary jobs at common labor. She worked for a while as a nanny for six children, but most often she, and sometimes her husband at the time, were migrant farm laborers. She worked long hours in the field and then labored over her typewriter late into the early morning hours. These are the bare bones of her life. According to the editor of her posthumously published autobiography, Jay Miller,

> Little has been recorded about her life. What is available includes fictions she created to protect her privacy. Intent on being a novelist, Christine [Mourning Dove] wove such fictions, usually quite plausible, into her work.[10]

There are some minor confluences between Mourning Dove and Erdrich, but only minor ones, and many differences between this first American Indian woman novelist and Erdrich. Erdrich is of mixed White and American Indian ancestry, while both Mourning Dove's parents were American Indian. Although not born into wealth, neither was Erdrich's early life one of desperate poverty and deprivation. Erdrich, coming from a family where both parents were teachers, had excellent educational opportunities and encouragement to go on to higher education, while Mourning Dove had to defend her desire, against her family's wishes, for even the most basic education. Erdrich had the two most important things that Mourning Dove lacked: education and a supportive family and that has made a great difference in their respective literary production.

Mourning Dove wrote *Cogewea* in 1912, but it would not see publication until 1927, nor would she receive any great economic or critical acclaim for the work. On the contrary, she continued to struggle economically, while her family and community refused to honor her work. Miller reports that,

> When her only novel seemed near release, local newspapers made public her ambitions. Her neighbors, both white and Indian grew suspicious, even hostile. When she later became politically active, some white reservation officials were critical of her, striking at her most heartfelt aspiration: they denied her literary ability. An agency farmer . . . said she had not written the novel but only allowed her name to appear on the work of a white man.[11]

Her novel made few ripples at the time of its publication and soon disappeared until it was reprinted in 1981 when injustices against American Indian and all things relating to Indians were brought to the forefront of American consciousness as a result of the civil rights movements and American Indian political activism in the late 1960s and early 1970s.

The women who are brave and strong enough to risk being the first at anything rarely achieve great personal success, but they make it a little easier for the next woman to step forward. Erdrich may or may not have been aware of Mourning Dove when she first felt the urge to write for publication, but Mourning Dove is widely honored by all American Indian women writers for her literary achievement and courage against all odds.

Roughly contemporary with Mourning Dove's publication of *Cogewea* was the African American writer Zora Neale Hurston (1891–1960). As part of the Harlem Renaissance of the 1920s, Hurston "arrived in Harlem in 1925 and came to symbolize the very heart and life of the movement . . . When she died in 1960 she had published more books than any other black American woman; yet she died in a welfare home, alone, forgotten, and penniless."[12] Born into the all-black town of Eatonville, Florida, Hurston was one of eight children with a Baptist preacher father who was distant and uninvolved with his family. After her mother's death, when Hurston was about 11 years old, the child was sent to live with one relative after another, but she still had the strength of will to enter and complete college. When one of her short stories, "Drenched in Light," was published, she moved to Harlem to pursue a literary career. Entering Barnard College, her career took a double path. Besides being a gifted writer, she also worked with the anthropologist Franz Boas, which probably inspired her to study and record the oral traditions of her own African American community in Florida. Her most well-known work is probably *Their Eyes Were Watching God,* which is a loosely organized novel that defies categorizing, as it employs extensive folk humor in places while compressing the narrative in others. By the time *Dust Tracks on a Road,* her autobiography, was published in 1942, her audience had almost evaporated. The civil rights movements of the 1960s and women's activist movements of the 1970s revived her work and introduced her to new readers. Now, she is appreciated as both an important black writer and an important woman of the 20th century.

A long arid period stretched between Hurston, Mourning Dove, and the next women writers of color, although there were African American men such as Langston Hughes, Richard Wright, Ralph Ellison, and James Baldwin who successfully published. Some American Indian men also wrote and published, including D'Arcy McNickle (Métis) who wrote and published novels such as *The Surrounded* (1936), *Runner in the Sun* (1954), and *Wind From an Enemy Sky* (1978). His novels were entertaining and while they were didactic, they did not rise to the level of tedious and off-putting preachiness that McWhorter had inserted into the narrative of Mourning Dove's *Cogewea.* According to Dorothy Parker, while he was a writer "largely by choice, he was a Native American who sought to restore pride and self determination to all Native American people."[13]

Of course, the most critically successful American Indian writer after 1969 was a man, N. Scott Momaday (Kiowa) who won the Pulitzer Prize for his novel, *House Made of Dawn.* He was followed by another man, James Welch (Black Feet/Gros Ventre), who in 1971 published *Riding the Earth Boy 40,* a collection of poems followed by the novel *Winter in the Blood* in 1974. Welch went on to publish a total of three books of poetry, five novels, and one nonfiction work about the Battle of the Little Big Horn from the Indian perspective, which was made into a documentary film. While Welch was busy with his early publications, women of color were also beginning to find entry into the literary world: Leslie Marmon Silko, of Laguna Pueblo, Mexican American, and White heritage was one of these women.

Silko's first foray into the literary world was a short story, "The Man to Send Rain Clouds," but like Erdrich and many other American Indian writers, her primary writing focus during those early years of 1968–1974 was poetry. Her first book publication was a collection of her early poems, *Laguna Women: Poems,* which was released from Greenfield Press in 1974. At only 35 pages, it was small but promising. Her first novel, and arguably her most notable achievement, was *Ceremony* published in 1977. This book is the one most often included as a course text for college classes in American Indian Literature. Over the course of her career, she would publish three nonfiction books, two more novels, and six more books that were either poetry or a combination of poetry, short stories, and a memoir, *The Turquoise Ledge* (2011). Her work began before Erdrich's, but continued simultaneously, and while the careers of the two women are those most often compared, their writing styles are very different.

Silko's writing is chunky and disjointed, which does not mean it is bad writing, only different in style from Erdrich's work. Silko's narratives rarely follow a linear time line but jumps backward and forward in time, often confusing readers who are accustomed to the Euro-western, straight forward, time sequential style. It takes some thinking or coaching to realize that Silko is using blank space on the page, italicized words, different type fonts, and center justification at times rather than right or left margins to signal these time shifts in the story. This style has often been compared to the postmodernist style of Kurt Vonnegut or Thomas Pynchon, but despite some similarities, postmodernism and Silko's American Indian style of writing had different origins. Silko's writing arose from the closer proximity of her heritage to oral tradition rather than literacy. Postmodernism was a reaction to the chaotic and confusion of modern society post–World War II, and some would argue, Post–World War I, when nothing seemed stable and reliable. Erdrich follows a more conventional Euro-western writing style in format, using word signals within the narrative to alert readers of time shifts, and usually, chapter breaks to indicate a change of narrator.

There were some people who thought they smelled a rivalry between Silko and Erdrich when Silko published a less than flattering review of Erdrich's *The Beet Queen*. Silko labeled the work as less than authentic, which caused dismay and hand-wringing, and possibly, hand rubbings of glee among people who might enjoy a literary feud. Erdrich quickly and graciously defused the situation with a few words, and the issue was dropped.[14] It is unknown if the two ever met in person.

The African American writer Alice Walker also began her literary career early in the 1970s, publishing poetry followed with short stories and then two novels: *The Life of Grange Copeland* (1970), followed by *Meridian* (1976). While working as an editor for *Ms Magazine*, Walker wrote an article for that publication about Zora Neale Hurston, which helped revived interest in Hurston's writing. Walker and Hurston had similar family backgrounds. Walker, like Hurston, had seven siblings, was born very poor in the rural south, and grew up hearing oral tradition stories. In 1982, she published her third novel, *The Color Purple,* which won her the Pulitzer Prize, and was made into a successful film directed by Stephen Spielberg in 1985. Set in the 1930s South, the book is a graphic depiction of life for young black women enduring not only White racism but also black patriarchy. Even with all the critical acclaim that the book and movie earned, the novel was one of the most frequently challenged books from 2000–2009 on the list maintained by the American Library Association. According to their website, "The ALA's Office of Intellectual Freedom (OIF) receives reports from libraries, schools, and the media on attempts to ban books in communities across the country."[15] Walker has continued her writing career with more novels, but she has also been and continues to be a political activist. She has not won as many writing awards as has Erdrich, but she has won the most important one in American letters, the Pulitzer.

Toni Morrison is another African American woman who began her writing career in the decade of the 1970s. Born into a working-class family in Ohio, Morrison started her life as Chloe Ardelia Wofford. Like Erdrich, she had a storyteller in the family, but it was her father, rather than her grandfather, who told her folk stories and legends that would find their way into Morrison's novels. A graduate of Howard University, Morrison went on to earn an M.A. from Cornell University in 1955, then to work as a text book editor for Random House. Her first novel, *The Bluest Eye,* was published in 1970, followed by *Song of Solomon* in 1975, and *Beloved* in 1987. This last novel earned her the Pulitzer Prize. *Jazz* came out in 1992, and in 1993, Morrison earned the highest literary prize possible: the Nobel. Like Erdrich, Morrison has also published children's books and nonfiction works, but unlike Erdrich, Morrison's novels do not start out as short stories. Indeed, that is one kind of writing that Morrison has eschewed with the exception of one short story, "Recitatif" published in 1983 in *Confirmation: An Anthology of African American Women.*[16]

Rudolfo Anaya was one of the earlier Chicano writers to break into the publishing world with his widely acclaimed first novel, *Bless Me Ultima,* in 1972. Born in Mexico, his family moved to New Mexico in the early 1950s where Anaya graduated from public schools, then went to business school for two years before enrolling at the University of New Mexico and earning his degree there. He taught public school while working on his first novel, and later became a professor in the English Department at the University of New Mexico. Acclaimed as the father of Chicano literature, Anaya would eventually publish 13 novels and 10 children's books. One of the wedge authors, Anaya's success paved the way for other Chicano/a authors such as Sandra Cisneros.

Cisneros's first book was a tiny chapbook of only seven poems, *Bad Boys* (1980). Her next book, the short novel (just over 100 pages), *The House on Mango Street,* was published in 1984. The novel is semi-autobiographical about a young girl growing up in Chicago. Told in vignettes, the style is somewhat similar to Erdrich's in that this is not the usual linear plot with one theme leading the reader from chapter to chapter, but a burst of stories that expand outward in multiple directions. She followed the novel with a collection of short stories, *Woman Hollering Creek and Other Stories.* The stories here epitomize Latino culture, especially for Latinas with stories of love, marriage, and children among other issues. She went on to publish two more collections of poetry: *My Wicked, Wicked Ways* (1992) and *Loose Women* (1995), and another novel, *Caramelo* (2003), as well as a children's book, *Hairs/Pelitos* (1997). Her work has become essential reading in college Chicano literature classes.

Julia Alvarez's books have been published contemporaneously with the works of Cisneros. Alvarez, a Dominican American Latina published her first novel, *How The Garcia Girls Lost Their Accents* in 1991, followed that one with another novel, *In the Time of Butterflies* in 1994. During the course of her writing career, she has published five novels, three collections of poetry, nine children's books, and three nonfiction works. The body of work by Latino/a writers and the number of these writers is destined to grow as more mainstream readers discover the richness and depth of these works and as the demographic of Latinos in the United States expands.

Chickasaw writer Linda Hogan began her literary career by publishing a chapbook of poetry, *Calling Myself Home,* in 1978 following up that work with five more books of poetry before publishing her first novel, *Mean Spirit,* in 1990. Since then, she has published three more novels: *Solar Storms, Power,* and *People of the Whale,* as well as five additional books of poetry and two works of creative nonfiction. She has won multiple awards for her work, which is narrowly focused on righting wrongs against American Indians and on environmental themes, which may be why she has not Erdrich's appeal to a wider reading audience. Still, she has done worthy writing that is often included in American Indian Literature classes. An academic herself, she has taught in creative writing and ethnic studies programs at the University of Colorado and at the University of Oklahoma.

Other American Indian women writers around the same time as Silko and Erdrich in the late 1970s and early 1980s are poets Joy Harjo (Creek), Luci Tapahonso (Navajo), and Ofelia Zepeda (Tohono O'odham), and of these, Harjo is the most prolific with 12 books of poetry to her credit. All three of these writers had and continue to have academic careers, as well. Harjo has ventured outside poetry to write several plays, and Zepeda is perhaps better known for her linguistics and language preservation work. She published a dictionary and grammar of her native language entitled *A Papago Grammar* (1983). Tapahonso, however, has kept strictly to her chosen poetry genre. While all three of these outstanding writers have earned their places in the literary field, none has gotten the public attention, literary awards and honors, and commercial success of either Silko or Erdrich.

Outside the continental United States, Velma Wallis (Athabaskan) from Alaska has two books to her credit, *Two Old Women* (1993), and *Bird Girl and the Man who Followed the Sun* (1996), both literary versions of oral tradition stories from her own tribe. Like many such native stories, these two books are narratives intended to foster courage and resourcefulness.

Among writers of Asian ancestry in America, the Chinese American author, Amy Tan, is perhaps the most well-known. Her first novel, *The Joy Luck Club* (1989) was largely autobiographical about her mother's first marriage to a brutal man and their children in World War II China, her coming to America and second marriage, then a return to China to rediscover her first family. Five other novels followed, including *The Kitchen God's Wife* (1991), two children's books, and three nonfiction works.

South Asian women have also contributed their share to the literary world, including Bapsi Sidhwa, who was born in Pakistan. Her first novel, *Cracking India* (1991), chronicles the story of people who had been lifelong neighbors and acquaintances turning against each other in an orgy of violence when Pakistan was partitioned from India. Sidhwa states, "Those were very tumultuous times and very cruel times, and I'm showing how man's nature changes into something very bestial when savage things happen."[17] Sidhwa would go on to write another five novels.

Thrity Umrigar, born in Bombay, India, was a journalist for 17 years, writing for such publications as the *Washington Post* and the *Cleveland Plain Dealer*. A teacher of creative writing at Case Western Reserve University, she has written a memoir, *First Darling of the Morning* (2004) as well as three novels, of which her best known work is *The Space Between Us* (2006).

Two other American Indian women have published novels since the turn of the millennium. In 2002, Debra Magpie Earling published *Perma Red,* and in 2006 Frances Washburn published *Elsie's Business.* Both of these novels address questions of violence, particularly violence against women. Washburn has published one more novel, *The Sacred White Turkey* (2010) and a third novel, *The Red Bird All-Indian Traveling Band* is under contract. Both women are academics, Earling at the University of Montana in Missoula and Washburn at the University of Arizona in Tucson.

Most of the American Indian women writers began their literary endeavors writing poetry, perhaps because that is a more accessible medium; poems can be written in short bursts. Each poem is usually a complete thought that needs no further elaboration, and can be put into a collection to make a book. Short stories require a more continuous effort, but the form stands alone, and like poetry, short stories can be arranged within a collection or revised and connected, as Erdrich has done into a longer narrative. Novels, on the other hand, require a sustained effort, often of years, and such lengths of time are a luxury that many American Indian women writers simply do not have available when they must earn a living and care for a family. Few have the determination and stamina to labor for years at a novel, as Mourning Dove did, while enduring poverty, ill health, bad relationships, and the disdain of others. Lucky is the woman like Erdrich who has early success and financial backing so that she can devote the necessary amount of time to creating longer pieces of writing.

At the time of this writing in the spring of 2013, it seems that few American Indian women are writing for publication, whether in the genre of poetry, short stories, novels, or creative nonfiction. There are American Indian men who continue literary careers, of which Sherman Alexie is the most notable. He and Erdrich are probably the two most recognizable names in American Indian literature. Alexie has more than 20 books to his credit—poetry, short stories, and novels, and two films derived from his work. Both have achieved commercial and critical success.

For more than 25 years, Cherokee writer Robert J. Conley has quietly but continuously published short stories and novels without the commercial success and fanfare that Erdrich and Alexie have received. Partly, this lesser-known quality may be because Conley's work has until recently been published by an academic press through the University of Oklahoma rather than through commercial presses. Academic publishers have less money to promote their authors' works than do the commercial publishers such as Harper Collins, but an advantage of publishing through an academic press is that authors' works are kept in print longer, which gives such books the opportunity to gain acceptance and sales over a period of time. Usually, commercial presses drop authors whose book sales do not meet rather high sales quotas. Further, academic publishers are usually more willing to look at what might be termed niche writing, while commercial presses want to publish books that have a broad appeal, and thus, higher sales.

Conley's work is mostly historical crime fiction set in the particular time just before and after the Cherokee Removal from the eastern United States via the Trail of Tears in 1836–1837 to Oklahoma Territory. His writing is tight; his characters, both the historical ones and the invented supportive actors, are finely drawn and well-rounded, and his plots are historically accurate. One of his more innovative books is *Mountain Windsong: A Novel of the Trail of Tears* (1992). The main character is a child who is the recipient of historical information conveyed by his grandfather, but Conley supports the grandfather's stories by including accurate historical sources such as letters from prominent figures contemporary with Cherokee Removal and the full text of treaties between the Cherokee Nation and the U.S. government.

Another more recent Cherokee novelist is Tom Holm, whose first novel, *The Osage Rose: An Osage Country Mystery* (2008), was another book from an academic publisher, which means it did not get the publicity that the work deserved. Also historical fiction, Holm himself calls the work a "who-dun-it."[18] The book details the results of three separate events from the 1920s: the Volstead Act, which ushered in prohibition, the Tulsa race riot of 1921, which killed more African Americans than any other similar event in American history, and the Osage Oil murders, where Osage and other American Indians of Oklahoma were murdered for the ownership of their oil-rich land. Holm's work, too, is tightly written with believable, complex characters—of White, African American, Osage, and Cherokee origins—and grounded in historical accuracy. *The Osage Rose* is his first novel, but Holm, had previously published academic books and articles about American Indian historical situations, such as *The Great Confusion in Indian Country: Native Americans and Whites in the Progressive Era* (2005), and *Strong Hearts, Wounded Souls: Native American Veterans of the Vietnam War* (1996). A sequel to *The Osage Rose* is in production.

David Treuer is another Ojibwe novelist like Erdrich, but from Leech Lake Reservation, rather than from Erdrich's Turtle Mountain. His three novels, *Little* (1996), *The Hiawatha* (1999), and *The Translation of Dr. Appelles: A Love Story* (2006), were critically well-received, but did not attain great commercial success. These stories, like Erdrich's, feature both White and Ojibwe characters, but the overall tone of the work is darker, with almost none of the humor that Erdrich employs to lighten even the darkest story. Treuer won the Pushcart Prize, and his books have been editor's picks from major newspapers, but none of the major prizes have come his way.

Erdrich has won every major American literary award with the exception of the highest, the Pulitzer Prize, which still eludes her, but may be in her future. Her work has been and continues to be critically and commercially successful, but perhaps it is the commercial success that has denied her the Pulitzer. There are still some critics who are of the notion that if writers are commercially successful then they cannot also be "good" writers, worthy of enshrinement with the greats, even though Erdrich's work has often been compared to Faulkner. Starving in a garret may not be a requisite for the highest literary acclaim, but it helps. Even some native writers have dismissed Erdrich as "commercial, mere popular fiction." Erdrich has committed the dual sins of appealing to the masses and making money, something that Hemingway, at least, of the decorated greats also did, but was forgiven, possibly because he was a man.

The Pulitzer is the highest American literary award, but the Nobel is the highest honor in the world, and that seems out of reach for Erdrich at this time considering the mood of the prize committee for the Nobel. In an Associated Press interview in 2008, Horace Engdahl, the permanent secretary of the Swedish Academy that hands out the Nobel Prizes in Literature stated:

> Of course, you can't get away from the fact that Europe is the center of the literary world, not the United States . . . The U.S. is too isolated, too insular. They don't translate enough and don't really participate in the big dialogue of literature. That ignorance is restraining.[19]

Toni Morrison, an African American woman, was the last American who won the Nobel Prize (1993). The academy has in the past given the award to writers who wrote in detail about situational events within their own countries—subjects that would have held little interest for people not of those nations, except that those events were coincidentally part of greater trends in the world. V. S. Naipaul, for instance, wrote novels of Asian people in the Caribbean, and how many people in the larger world are unaware that there are descendants of migrants from the Asian subcontinent who have long resided in places like Trinidad. How much more insular and narrow could a writer's subject be than a novel about a man of east Indian descent named Biswas desiring to buy a house in Trinidad, and the comedy of manners of his life?[20] Naipaul's work happened to coincide with larger world issues regarding social distance of class, of the desire to belong and to fit into a preconceived notion of what it means to be successful. Undoubtedly, Naipaul's work is of the highest quality and deserving of recognition, but it was not lack of quality that the Swedish Academy cited as evidence for failing to consider any American authors for the 2008 Nobel Prize in Literature.

However, to ignore world writers of color in juxtaposition with the work of Erdrich might fulfill Engdall's claim that Americans are "too isolated, too insular." There are many writers of color—both men and women—producing outstanding work that might be at least in the pool of potential nominees for a Nobel Prize along with Erdrich.

Ngugi wa thiong'o, a Nigerian writer of Gikuyu ethnicity, is one of the best known African writers producing novels, plays, poetry, critical works, and a memoir, *Dreams in a Time of War* (2011). His writing career has spanned close to 60 years, beginning with the publication of his novel, *Weep Not, Child* in

1964, and continuing with five other novels and multiple articles and critical works. His writing illustrates the colonial experience of African Indigenous people, their struggles for independence and efforts to end corruption in their new states. Ngugi invented the concept of decolonization of the mind, which has been adopted and adapted by Indigenous people around the world.

Chinua Achebe, also of Nigeria but of Igbo ethnicity rather than Gikuyu like Ngugi, is probably the mostly widely read African author, particularly well known for his novel, *Things Fall Apart* (1958), which has become a standard text book for high school literature courses as well as at the university level. This book accurately details the devastating effect of Christian missionizing efforts in an African Indigenous community. Eerily, it closely parallels the American Indian experience with Christian missionaries as well as that of Canadian First Nations. A prolific writer, Achebe has 31 published books that include novels, poetry, short story collections, critical works, and children's stories, all of which draw upon his oral tradition roots. Nobel watchers have speculated for years that Achebe would win the prize, but not so far.

Nigeria seems to produce some of Africa's best writers from multiple ethnic roots. Amos Tutuola was a Nigeria from the Yoruba tribe, the son of cocoa farmers, who only achieved six years of school, yet wrote and published multiple works that, like Achebe and Ngugi, drew upon folk tales and oral traditions. His first novel is *The Palm Wine Drinkard* (1952), and he published at least 11 more books of stories. He died in 1997 at the age of 76.

Buchi Emecheta, as an Igbo Nigeria woman writer, chronicles the experience of Black African women, both in Nigeria and in the diasporic world of England. Her first published work was the novel, *In the Ditch* (1972), and she has followed that with more than 20 additional novels, plays, children's books, and her autobiography, *Head Above Water*. Emecheta has said that she sees the future of literature in Africa as being in the hands of African women, "because, they, as modern women, are combining the slave tongue [English] . . . with an African consciousness. . . . Women are carriers of cultures in whatever language."[21]

On the other side of the world, two New Zealand Indigenous writers from the Maori tribe, Witi Ihimaera and Patricia Grace, have contributed their work to the world of literature. Ihimaera has published 15 novels and 17 short story collections. His most famous work is probably *The Whale Rider* (1987), which was made into a successful movie in 2003 in spite of a cast of mostly unknowns. The story is classic, a girl who is traditionally excluded from positions of power because of her sex, fights to overcome prejudice to become a leader, but there are no clichés here. Ihimaera's family and social conflicts are real and believable.

Patricia Grace in 1975 published the first collection of short stories, by a Maori woman, *Waiariki*. She went on to publish seven more collections of short stories, three children's books, and six novels, including *Potiki* (1986). Her work, like that of fellow Maori Ihimaiera and the African writers, Achebe, Ngugi, Tutuola, and Emecheta draws upon her Indigenous culture and storytelling as well as the experience of colonized subjectivity.

North across the medicine line, among others, Eden Robinson is a relatively young (born in 1968) First Nations woman writer of Haisla and Heiltsuk heritage. Her first book was *Traplines* (1996), a critically acclaimed collection of four longer than usual short stories. Perhaps, she is naturally more comfortable with narratives longer than the short story because her next two books are both novels, *Monkey Beach* (2000) and *Blood Sports* 2006). The best known is *Monkey Beach* with a young adult main character who tells the story in flashbacks of her brother's disappearance and the search for him, while also revealing the family history that contributed to the brother's disappearance. References to Elvis Presley, an uncle who is an old hippie, a mystical grandmother, and a mother who disbelieves in the unseen spirits, all contribute to a story of trauma and healing set on the northwest coast of Canada. Themes here will resonate with Erdrich readers. There is youthful (and adult!) promiscuity, family and community violence, secrets and indiscretions as well as the underlying theme of a people still enduring and working to overcome the effects of colonization.

All of these writers of color, men and women, not only from America but from Indigenous populations on multiple continents have contributed their words to the body of human knowledge, enriching the lives of those of us who read. And one of the main themes for many of these writers is the effects of colonization, its continuance in some places, and the postcolonial condition in others.

That same theme runs throughout all of Erdrich's work in the situation of American Indians pre-contact times, in the traditional post-contact past, and in the modern era. That is not an isolationist, America-only theme, but representative of the history and continuing saga of Indigenous people from Africa and Asia, North and South America, New Zealand and Australia, and points in between. Her work resonates with readers, learned and barely lettered, not only in the United States, but around the world. She writes the stories of injustice and of the urge to right wrongs of the past while living and thriving in the present; her work is about the humanity and inhumanity inherent within everyone, and the depths and heights of emotion that are not distinctly American, but universal. It may be that a future Swedish Academy will recognize the error of their thinking. It may be simply that Erdrich's time has not yet come for a Nobel, or even a Pulitzer.

Commercially, Erdrich is one of the most successful authors of any nationality, race, ethnicity, or gender. Her books continue to sell, from *Jacklight* and *Love Medicine* to *The Porcupine Year* and *The Round House*. She continues to win awards, to pack people in for her readings, and to be asked to speak at significant events. Many authors make only a modest living, if that, from royalties on their books. The "real" money comes from selling the rights for a film production, or creating their own film of one or more of their novels, but that has not happened for Erdrich, as it did for Sherman Alexie. Her writing simply does not lend itself well to screenplays. Erdrich's work contains a great deal of narrative rather than dialogue—information provided by the author directly to the reader or through the inner thoughts of the characters, which is difficult to translate into film, where the viewer can only grasp what is said by the actors or the actions performed without words. Getting inside the mind of the character/actors (when her work is translated to stage or film) can only be achieved by having them speak their thoughts aloud, or by having a narrative voice-over, which was one of the problems Marsha Norman encountered when converting *The Master Butcher's Singing Club* into a stage production. In order to get across ideas and information that Erdrich provided in the narration, Norman had to enlist an actor to step out of character and speak directly to the audience. That rarely works. Audience members feel like children or students being lectured by a parent or a teacher rather than seeing a story unfold naturally before their eyes. Someone may yet successfully translate one or more of Erdrich's novels to the stage or screen, but if that never happens, Erdrich will not be hurt financially.

Twenty years after Erdrich was chosen by *People* magazine as one of the 100 most beautiful people, she was again on public view as one of 12 renowned Americans chosen as subjects for the television program, *Faces of America*, on PBS.[22] The show examined the genealogy and contributions to America society of 12 Americans from Erdrich to Yo Yo Ma. Gates and his staff researched the family history of each participant, which for Erdrich included both the German and Ojibwe strands of her heritage. Among other issues, Erdrich discussed why ancestral history is central to the existence of Native Americans; self-identity and her grandfather's influence on whether or not she belonged in her tribal nation; and her grandfather's role against the federal government policy of terminating their relationship to tribes and their status within the United States in the 1950s. The episode proved not only that Erdrich is still a public figure, but provided an opportunity to educate the general American viewer about the historical, political, and economic positioning of American Indians, as well as proving that 20 years after the *People Magazine* appearance, Louise Erdrich is still beautiful in mind, body, and soul.

Her readers will continue to be delighted whenever she releases a new novel or collection of short stories or poetry, and she will gain new readers who appreciate her, and lucky they are for they will have the joy of reading not only the novel they just found, but all her preceding work as well, a feast of letters. As one of the most prolific American writers, and American Indian writers, there is every reason to believe she has more stories yet to tell and much more family life to enjoy with her daughters, her extended family, and friends.'

NOTES

1. Olwen Hufton, *The Prospect Before Her: A History of Women in Western Europe, 1500–1800* (New York: Alfred A. Knopf, Inc., 1995).

2. Ibid., 424.

3. Ibid., 361–423.

4. Ibid., 431.

5. See Billy J. Stratton, *Buried in Shades of Night: Contested Voices, Indian Captivity, and the Legacy of King Philip's War,* Tucson: University of Arizona Press, 2013.

6. *The Norton Anthology of American Literature, Third Ed.* (New York: W. W. Norton, 1979), 49–50.

7. Ibid., 240.

8. See Frances Washburn, "Zitkala Sa: Bridge Between Two Worlds," in *Their Own Frontier: Women Intellectuals Re-Visioning the American West,* eds. Shirley Anne Leckie and Nancy J. Parezo (Lincoln: University of Nebraska Press, 2008).

9. Mourning Dove [Hum-ishu-ma], *Cogewea the Half-Blood* (Boston: Four Seas Co., 1927. Reprint Lincoln: University of Nebraska Press, 1981. First Bison Book Printing, Lincoln: University of Nebraska Press, 1991).

10. Jay Miller, *Mourning Dove: A Salishan Autobiography* (Lincoln: University of Nebraska Press, 1190), xii.

11. Ibid.

12. *The Norton Anthology of American Literature,* 1940.

13. Dorothy R. Parker, Back cover, *Singing an Indian Song: A Biography of D'Arcy McNickle* (Lincoln: University of Nebraska Press, 1992).

14. Leslie Marmon Silko, "Book Review of Louise Erdrich's *The Beet Queen,*" *Impact: Albuquerque Journal Magazine,* October 7, 1986 (Reprint: *Studies in American Indian Literature.* V10.4, Fall 1986): 177.

15. American Library Association Banned Books website, www.ala.org/advocacy/banned/aboutbannedbooks.

16. Amiri and Amina Baraka, eds., *Confirmation: An Anthology of African American Women* (New York: Morrow, 1983).

17. Feroza Jussawalla and Reed Way Dasenbrock, eds., *Interviews with Writers of the Post-Colonial World* (Jackson: University Press of Mississippi, 1992).

18. Author conversation with Tom Holm, May 9, 2012.

19. Aislinn Simpson, *The Telegraph,* October 8, 2008, www.telegraph.co.uk/news/worldnews/northamerica/USA/Nobel-literature-prize-judge-Americans-authors-insular-and-ignorant.html.

20. V. S. Naipaul, *A House for Mr. Biswas* (New York: Alfred A. Knopf, 1961).

21. Jussawalla and Dasenbrock, eds., *Interviews,* 99.

22. Henry Louise Gates, Jr., *Faces of America.* PBS, February 10–March 3, 2010. www.pbs.org/wnet/faces of america/profiles/louise-erdrich/10/.

TEN

Conclusions

Twenty-eight years after Louise Erdrich published her first two books, her work continues to impress and delight readers and critics alike, and her life continues to be a source of interest, even fascination. Why is this true, when some other writers of any ancestry, no matter how much their work is appreciated, are usually just the names on the book, the names that appreciative readers may search for on bookseller's websites and shelves for those authors' latest works? And to speak more narrowly, why have so few other women writers of color or specifically American Indian women writers, achieved the level of public acclaim and commercial success as Erdrich has done? Being physically beautiful has not hurt her, but then, Stephen King has achieved comparable popular success and no one would call him beautiful. Other American Indian women writers are also far more than marginally attractive, beautiful many would say; yet, their work has not achieved the critical and commercial success that Erdrich's has. Many factors have weighed in Erdrich's favor, not the least of which is talent with a healthy seasoning of luck.

Erdrich was first a poet, and because that medium is so spare, poets have to know words and consider the impact that each word will have on the reader or listener. She carried that finely tuned sensibility over into her prose writing using words that not only move a plot line forward, but appeal to the senses of sight, sound, smell, and touch—words that are not so descriptive or distracting of themselves to slow down the plot but enough to make the reader more acutely aware of the journey they are taking from the first words of a novel to the end. Well-chosen words are all well and good, but Erdrich's subject matter is a factor as well.

She writes of the culture collision between American Indian societies and Euro-American colonizers, a story 500 plus years old, but largely ignored in the history classes taught in American public schools. Other writers have written on the same subject matter, but even in the 21st century often those stories are set up in binaries—us versus them, savage versus civilized, saints versus sinners, ecologists versus despoilers—which serve to inflame passions rather than to increase cross-cultural understanding of history. Erdrich addresses historical injustice, yes, but she complicates and explicates presenting nuanced stories that are closer to truth, if there is such a thing as one single truth. She creates bad actors and good actors on both sides and some of her characters are both good and bad all in one person.

The geographical settings for her stories are mostly in the upper Great Plains/Great Lakes region of the United States, an area often overlooked in American literature.[1] The number of novels set in New York or Los Angeles or some other urban area are legion; perhaps readers think of cities as vibrant and full of history and life simply because more people live there. The people of small town and rural America, however, have made important, often-ignored contributions to the social, economic, and political life of the United States. Some beloved authors have written into the same settings as Erdrich—Willa Cather, Laura Ingalls Wilder, and, more recently, Jane Smiley. While their texts may illuminate, they are also noticeable for what they obscure—the Native American experience that is foundational to the region. Erdrich's work, however, presents the most multidimensional stories of this region of any writer to date, with all the courage of the pioneer planting crops and surviving against the weather, and of dispossessed American Indians fighting for their land and their survival, and finally, for their recognition and dignity. Erdrich speaks for both groups, but especially for the American Indian voice declaring in the words of the Neil Diamond song, "I am, I said/I am, said I."[2]

While she writes stories of a region, they are not regional or provincial, or insular or even distinctly American isolationist as the Swedish Academy for the Nobel Prize would have the world believe. Her stories are everywhere and everyone's stories because her characters are imbued with universal human qualities. Every reader can recognize himself or herself in the throes of first love and lust such as Fleur and Eli experience in *Tracks,* or the desire for revenge that Fleur feels in *Four Souls,* or the sanctimonious behavior that Pauline displays in *Tracks.* Readers recognize themselves or people they have known, but unable to put those experiences into words, they/we are grateful that Erdrich can do that for us.

For 28 or more years, Erdrich has sustained her writing effort, continued to produce from her experience and imagination and research, tales of wonder that demonstrate our humanity and inhumanity, make us think, or allow us the repose to not think at all. We are grateful for the gift.

In her own words:

Once we were a people who left no tracks. Now we are different. We print our-
selves deeply on the earth. We build roads. The ruts and skids of our wheels bite
deep and the bush recedes. We make foundations for our buildings and sink
wells beside our houses. Our shoes are hard and where we go it is easy to follow. I have left my own tracks, too. I have left behind these words. But even as
I write them down I know they are merely footsteps in snow. They will be gone
by spring. New growth will cover them, and me. That green in turn will blacken,
snow will obscure us all, but, my sons and daughters, sorrow is a useless thing.
Much as the grass dies, the wind exhausts its strength, the tree topples in a light
breeze, the dead buffalo melt away into the prairie ground or are plowed into
newly scratched-out fields, all things familiar dissolve into strangeness. Even our
bones nourish change, and even a people who lived so close to the bone and were
saved for thousands of generations by a practical philosophy, even such people
as we, the Anishinaabeg, can sometimes die, or change, or change and become.[3]

NOTES

1. Recognizing that much of the rest of the country largely ignores the Great Plains
states of the upper Midwest, University of Nebraska Press has created a series of books
entitled "Flyover Fiction," referring, of course, to the notion that the rest of the country
simply flies over that region on their way from one coast to the other but never stops to
examine what great value lies within the region.

2. Neil Diamond, "I Am, I Said," Prophet Music (ASCAP), 1971.

3. Louise Erdrich, *Four Souls* (New York: First Harper Perennial Edition, 2005), 210.

Appendix

As a student at Dartmouth College, Louise Erdrich published one short story and four poems in three separate issues of *DART,* which was the literary magazine produced under the guidance of English Department faculty. At that time, Erdrich published under the name Karen Erdrich, rather than Louise Erdrich. As far as it is known, this is her first published writing. The following short story appeared in the Spring 1975 issue (*DART* 3.2):

Renny

I didn't want to touch it. It was snaking at me in the dream. Then I halfways woke in the dark cold, listening. Pa was breathing loud in the next room. Hot, sour roses on his breath last night. Ma whimpering and breaking something when he came home like that. I halfways began to think about getting up . . . Kettles got to be lit. It's donut day. Kettles got to be lit . . . Joby used to light the kettles, now I got to. Pretty soon I was up, my bare feet hit the linoleum. Jesus the water is cold in the morning. I won't sit on the toilet, just hold it till I warm up. My clothes, ice breathing ice on my skin, shivering. I walked downstairs to the shop to get the kettles lit—once Joby puked in the hot grease. Tater puffs. God that got around and you could bet it was bad for business. Oven. Flourbin. Slicer. Racks of bread and cake, all stale. Business is off. No money to fix the cracked window. Stuff in the window got to be changed, all crumbs. Mice been at it, got to arrange it nice . . . inviting. I couldn't see out the windows with the lights on so I never knew he was watching. My dress was just starting to get warm on me when I turnt the lights off.

Then I saw him watching black shadow the sky lighting up greenblue behind him.

I got empty inside, pounding. Then he was gone. All day that stuck in my mind like nothing else and at noon I told Mamma.

Oh god Renny don't bother me, just an old drunk.

Yeah Mamma, I said but he was watching.

Let Pa take care of him Renny, he's probably after old bread.

Probably, I said.

Pa came in then and looked at me funny like he always does but he didn't say nothing. So I didn't say nothing further on it, but sure as hell I wouldn't get up next morning because I just knew he'd be watching and it made me sick to think of him seeing me from the shadow when I couldn't see him back.

☙❧

Next morning I kept all the lights off at first and checked the window. But I didn't see nothing and then I thought I heard something in the back. I quick flipped on the lights. Shit, I said, what a baby. Joby would never be scared, not of a man in the dark. Joby would punch out anybody looked crossways at him. Only thing Joby was scared of is really hurting somebody when he got mad. Then I was just laughing to myself and lit up the kettles. Joby once punched out the mayor of the town who is a doctor, for personal satisfaction. He did it because the mayor's daughter was purely mean, nobody had business raising a child to be like that, Joby said. Also Joby once laid into the half-wit for calling him a dirty name but Leonard meant nothing by it and Joby felt bad after.

I brought up some old donuts, which ain't so bad before your taste memories wake up on you. That day there was to be an assembly. Fat Pam would wag her boobs at the boys sniggering behind me like I wasn't there. Dumb farmers, clods, thinking they they [sic] just knew it all. Well I got my little secrets. Jesus yes, more than they'll ever know about sex. I got on my coat and went out. I was cold already and I had a mile to go in the wind and cross the field.

The field was worse. I didn't usually think I could make it. I had to cross it because they set the new school out of town where the rich are building up. The wind pummeled at me and got up under my dress and sleeves and down my neck till I was cold inside as the wind. It was just me and that blazing white space. I thought of wolves. The sound they would make. I would hear it from the clump of trees. I used to play there when the big swing was hung from the lowest branch. I thought back to summer and pretended the wind rising gooseflesh on my back was the sun pricking me with heat. The trees were buzzing and the tire swing was taking me high into the clicking leaves. Joby gave me an underpush and I was there, touching the hot green tips with my toes.

☙❧

It was dark by the time I got out from school that day. On the way home I always went the long way past the cemetery. The burning statue of jesus christ [sic] stood in the middle of the dark pines and the fields of ice. The wind was crossways. I wasn't bucking it. It moved everything in the cemetery, the pines, the stones, the flickering statue, everything moved. It wasn't natural and I ran fast, passing the clump of pines at the end and I think I glimpsed a man in them. He stared from the thrashing branches. He had a long coat and something on his head. I couldn't hardly see his face. It blurred, I ran off and never stopped all the rest of the way home.

Mamma was mad at me being late. I was supposed to work right after school selling long johns and buns to people who had to buy things cheap. That was the only kind would buy in our bakery. The other bakery in town looked clean and hadn't a cracked front window. Their ways weren't no better than ours of baking. I knew. They were dirty in the back and just hid it better.

Pa was out back frying twist-ups and glazing them over. I ate a cream-filled and polished the glass thinking of Joby and how he went off in the army. Joby had a girl now, he showed me her picture and she sure was good looking in all the right places. Joby told me I was good looking too where it counted, I got a pretty face and long hair. Anyway, I ain't so bad. Personality counts too, they say. But lately I've got it out for nearly everybody at school.

I had almost forgot about the man but then as I was about to lock up, he came in. Stocking cap, the kind that covers up your face, I was scared to look through the eyes. I ran out on him before he stuck his hand out of his pocket. I ran upstairs. Pa came up just after. Mad but jesus [sic] he was mad. Looked at me like I was nothing he ever wanted to have around.

When you gonna grow up.

John, you lay off her, said Mamma.

But he didn't. He went on about how stupid I am. I got sick of it.

You ain't so smart yourself, I said.

He looked about to hit me.

Try it, buster, I said. You can't run even a bakeshop decent. You get drunk on Mamma's money. You never cared about me nor Joby. That's why he run off and I'm going too [sic] Damn fucker, I said. Damn you.

With that I run straight out neverminding [sic] the cold. I didn't have no jacket on but so what, I said, when I freeze he'll be pretty sorry for his girl. He used to call me his girl. I was going down to the park, to the warming house. I didn't have my skates but I had enough money to rent for an hour.

So I got down there and Virgin, who runs the counter, let me have his jacket and the skates for all night. Three hours solid I skated around the rink. Sometimes I'd square off and do curly eights. If there's one thing I do good, it's to skate. When I twirled I made my own wind about me in my ears. Some kids watched and wanted me to learn them hot to fancy stop so your skates make a long scratch in the ice. I showed them how to tip up on the stopperteeth [sic] and how to dip down on the blade edge. I went off, dancing through spotlights and flakes in the air, whirling like I was animalfree. [sic] I like to skate. I swooped low and fast, whistling against the wind I made. I never fell once, even when I jumped up to turn and land on one foot which is my specialty though hazardous.

The pond is fairly big. The boys play hockey at one end but the other is dark and willows hang over the edge. It was on the dark end I practiced my most experimental and dangerous tricks for then I was likely to fall.

I couldn't stay down there that night though, the man with the stocking cap was on my mind. I couldn't unstick the picture. I kept skating faster as I thought of him standing in his black coat and stocking cap, hands in his pockets and rubber overboots. . . . Standing there with his hands in his pocket and his black coat and his stocking cap. . . . and I kept going faster, then all the wind flew out of me.

I fell at the dark edge. I lay there looking at the stars twirling in sparkling arches like they was skating too.

Missy. Missy longhair. Pretty missy did you fall down little girly?

I heard it. I wanted to get up. I couldn't tell where it came from, the willows ere dark, they still had their leaves. The willows were black and rattling.

Pretty lamb, lamby longhair. . . . will you come in here and suck . . .

I can't hear it. I jumped up and skated. It was like I never learned how. I would gobble up the ice too fast then wobble and fall. The wind would rush and then it would stop. I finally got to the warming house. Virgin said he'd take me home but he never did. I waited around but he was so long cleaning up I was scared Pa would get even more sick angry. I couldn't sit still so I ran out. I was running home.

Then he was in front of me.
Then I was I don't know where He
Had it It was out He
hit me with it I was down.
cold. black. hot. knife. and he
had me with it and again he
had me with it It
had an eye and it looked all through me
and then it had a hand and it
took metill till till till till
there was nothing left but whiteness the wind
stopping the wolves blazing field
The stars skating Tipping off the edge stopping
The wind up in my clothes.
I had nothing to eat.
There was nothing to feed.
I couldn't walk.
There was nothing to walk with.
I was all saw inside
Everything had been taken out and looked at.

‟‟

Nobody could make me go to school for a while after that nor eat nor do anything I didn't want to do. I couldn't even do anything I wanted to do. I had begun to feel a slow rot in me starting from where he looked all through me and it spread, spread into my stomach.

Somedays all it would take was the pure, thin, tiddlywink of jesus [sic]. I begun to go to church every morning. I was no catholic but nevertheless I loved jesus [sic]. Jesus never had one. His mamma took it when he was born. He never looked inside a woman but to heal the slow rot she had inside her. Jesus was a sweet one.

The church was down the street from the bakeshop, past the stores and photograph studio. I went there after I lit up the kettles and sat in the place, quiet, warmflickering [sic]. Nobody came but old women in black and Leonard the half-wit with the thick bottom glasses.

Crows, they look like crows at the altar. The bright man comes in with the golden cups. He sings, they flap about him, he sings for blood. The bells ring seven times. Three times the dark birds in the pews touch their claws to their breasts. Crows sing in the loft. Stars turn on the pipes. Smokewater music Sun drowning in music. Dawn of bells and of windows. Ruby red for eyes, gold of gold and the black book and blue cloak and the pur tasteless Christ, blind inside me. It was almost as good as skating, walking down the aisle mouthing that floaty cracker.

And once as I sat there I knew I wouldn't be scared of stocking cap no more. Soon Joby would be home. All this time I waited for Joby because I knew he wouldn't let me down. No, I wouldn't be scared of stocking cap. I'd get what I could use to look through him like he done me. Joby would give it to me. His sweet little thirty-eight. He'd put it in my hand and show me how to work it. We'd go target shooting at tin cans and rabbits. I wouldn't shoot no rabbits. Joby, he can pick them off a near fifty feet. I don't care. I won't be out for no rabbits.

I'd find stocking cap some night but not by accident. I'd be watching and laying in wait. I'd shoot straight through the holes in his cap. He won't have no eyes to look through anything with. He'd die, I'd see his guts silt in the snow. Sorry. . . . he'd be sorry.

Sorry, it's too damn late. . . .

Sorry buddy boy, but. . . .

I'd level at him and press the trigger easy like Joby said. I'd let him have it.

Me and Joby, we'd go off. Maybe we'd sit in the church and fall asleep in the pews. The sun would fall on our faces and wake us, making us holy clowns. Skating red, blue, gold across our eyelids. We'd laugh like crazy. We'd hop a boxcar. We'd never come back.

෧෧

Then I thought this to myself. What if Joby don't give me the gun? He don't have to. He might not give me the gun.

෧෧

I come back to myself in the church and I looked at the candle in the glasses, burning and winking like bad, bright eyes. I looked at the christboy and he smiled. I smiled back and the mystery was on our lips. We knew I had weapons. Other weapons, secret and terrible. His mother smiled too. Her smile was like mine. Her hands were turning and gleaming in the light. The dawn was caught in her long, shining claws.

The following two poems appeared in *DART* 7.1 (Fall 1975, Winter 1976).

ODE TO HIGH SCHOOL SEX
In the many-handed night, the badboys run,
Pranking through iron and cozening hedges,
Or jack-backing bomb songs at the stopped front door
in dazzling fenders and lordly chrome.
And where are the goodgirls?
Trussed in their ruffles?
They are under the alders in blueblack plumes,
With sequins sneaking after they glances,
They ride the asparagus in dancing shoes.

And now they cry to the lightheeled boys,
and now they are tumbling like buckets of plums,

Awry in hayfields with stars on their tips.
Alive in backseats at frizzling speeds.

And not the poor knob with a pin on his name,
Not the frumpity girl with gum under her chin,
Will miss out on the fullness or the filling in.

Let ad-men proffer their magic cakes.
Let goat-eyed teachers hiss,
Let citizens render complaints to the mayor
and parents fume like whales—

We will leap into hills with joined up tails,
conspiring with spring. We will catch the drunk plums
on our coiled up tongues,
as the continent of winter sinks!
All tippling Ripple, we will tune our parts
to the damned band of love, the golden
dying of harvests.

NIGHT ON WARD B
I saw the simpleton rise up
in the light of the bar-sliced moon,
who shone full-face, her ancient lips
mouthing maddish tunes. The simpleton is silent,
though he does communicate
with chairs and television sets,
and knows the secret names of plants
and all their sins, for he
is confessor of a world of things.
And then the moon swung down
her wild and brittle hair, it fell
about the simpleton
in brilliant shades of light.
Ant that same night she made
delirious demands upon his tongue
and pressed herself against his teeth, till he
was forced to speak, aloud.
And speaking for the first time
he declared his love
that trembled in his breast
like the hand of a cloud.
For years! He said, it hung like a hawk'
longing to pluck
the nipples of the servant-girl, as they
so gently swayed to the sounds he made.
Two pearls. A feast. But she refused
Somehow, and he was wroth,

and lost in longing—he cut them off
to fondle in his pocket till they day
they changed, grew hooks, began to bleed—
and then he fed them moths
till they grew wings
and flew, pink and shivering, to her breasts again.
Yet, she never knew,
she shoved him down when he made signs
to her drunken buttons, shining,
shining in her shirt. He tried
he pressed his mouth
to give them air for they were blue
and dying, dying in the harness.
Though at night
She surely lets them out,
for they have come to visit him, all dark
and changed in form—
they have assumed the horns of lions
and of foul giraffes, and hissing like
the original snake, they dance
a lurid polka in his brain. Sometimes they strip,
and caper in their skins without their furs,
all purple veined and strenuously tipped,
with crimson and in broader hues, they twirl
in massive and extreme display, till he has
for his own sake
been forced to make them tame,
and he embraced, despite their claws,
panthers, and he French-kissed sharks
and taught them checkers.
Now they play
for hours, on the warm verandas of his face.

Yet there are nights when they rise
and stare
as the moon fills the garden
as she walks through the air,
as she ripples like water,
and he drowns in her hair.

The following two poems appeared in *DART* 4.3 (Spring 1976).

THE HINTERLANDS
Now and again, I think of the dawn-beaters
and see flames drumming at the world's rim.

When the sky pales and lengthens
and its cold ring of bone
vanished behind a cloud,
I remember my home.

Each year the harvesters, stiff with the salt dirt,
cover the land with stumps of bread.
When all is done and said.
The wheatshocks brush the black heavens
and the fences
shuffle beside the road like convicts.
The fields, turning in sleep, cry softly
and something stops in the shadow of a barn.

GRACE
London. The night's scum
on the milkbottles, pale numb choirs
with empty chests, suppressing
a collective breath till 7,
the miraculous

Day when I close and open books
from which dark fields spread
their lush rows
toward some mythic horizon
of the mind, I suppose.

I dream of my mother picking potatoes
as a young girl on the reservation.
When her back hurt, she stood up
level with a cloud of grit
that whirled in the distance.
Probably she blew into her hands
as I do now—near a drafty window
from which I see
two towers of copper verdigris

Between them, the moon may rise, it depends
on popular demand.
If it doesn't I'll rub my eyes
& thank the Queen for planning the surprise.

Bibliography

Achebe, Chinua. *Things Fall Apart*. Reprint. New York: Alfred A. Knopf, 1992.

Alvarez, Julia. *How the Garcia Girls Lost Their Accents*. New York: Plume, 1991.

Alvarez, Julia. *In the Time of Butterflies*. New York: Plume, 1994.

American Library Association website, www.ala.org/advocacy/banned/aboutbanned books.

Anaya, Rudolfo. *Bless Me Última*. Berkeley: TQA Publications, 1972.

Apess, William. *A Son of the Forest: The Experience of William Apess, A Native of the Forest, Comprising a Notice of the Pequod Tribe of Indians, Written by Himself*. Out of Print.

Baraka, Amiri, and Amina Baraka, eds. *Confirmation: An Anthology of African American Women*. New York: Morrow, 1983.

Barrow, John. "All the Right Connections/Louise Erdrich adds *Burning Love* to Other Related Tales." *Chicago Sun Times,* May 26, 1996.

Beidler, Peter G. "The Facts of Fictional Magic: John Tanner As a Source for Louise Erdrich's *Tracks* and *The Birchbark House*." *American Indian Culture and Research Journal* 24:4, 2000.

Birchbark Books website, Birchbarkbooks.com/ourstory. Book reviews. http: www. bookbrowse.com/reviews/.

Bronte, Anne. *The Tenant of Wildfell Hall*. Tyler: Arcturus Press, 2010.

Bronte, Charlotte. *Jane Eyre*. New York: Dover Publications, 2003.

Bronte, Emily. *Wuthering Heights*. New York: SoHo Books, 2012.

Brave Bird, Mary, with Richard Erdoes. *Ohitika Woman*. New York: Grove Press, 1993.

Brumble, David, III. *American Indian Autobiography*. Berkeley: University of California Press, 1988.

Charles, Ron. "Love in the Time of Bitterness." *The Washington Post,* Feb. 3, 2010.

Chavkin, Alan, and Nancy Fehl. *Conversations with Louise Erdrich and Michael Dorris*. Jackson: University Press of Mississippi, 1994.

Cisneros, Sandra. *Bad Boys*. London: Mango Publications, 1980.

Cisneros, Sandra. *Caramelo*. New York: Alfred A. Knopf, 2002.

Cisneros, Sandra. *Hairs/Pelitos*. Edmund: Dragonfly Publishers, 1997.

Cisneros, Sandra. *The House on Mango Street*. New York: Vintage, 1990.

Cisneros, Sandra. *Loose Women*. New York: Vintage, 1995.

Cisneros, Sandra. *My Wicked, Wicked Ways*. New York: Alfred A. Knopf, 1992.

Cisneros, Sandra. *Woman Hollering Creek*. New York: Vintage, 1992.

Cohen, Leah Hager. "Cruel Love." *The New York Times Sunday Book Review,* Feb. 5, 2010.

Combs, Marianne. "Why Is the Master Butcher's Singing Club Closing Early?" *MPR News,* Oct. 26, 2010.

Condon, Patrick. "Compelling 'Shadow Tag' a departure for Erdrich." *AP Worldstream,* Feb. 21, 2010.

Conley, Robert J. *Mountain Windsong: A Novel of the Trail of Tears*. Norman: University of Oklahoma Press, 1992.

Covert, Calvin. "The Anguished Life of Michael Dorris." *Minneapolis Star Tribune,* Aug. 2, 1997.

Croft, Georgia. "Something Ventured." White River Junction, VT: *Valley News,* Apr. 28, 1987.

Crow Dog, Mary, with Richard Erdoes. *Lakota Woman*. New York: Grove Press, 1990.

Dartmouth College website, http://.Dartmouth.edu/home/about/history/html.

Debo, Angie. *And Still the Waters Run: The Betrayal of the Five Civilized Tribes*. Princeton: Princeton University Press, 1940.

Deloria, Vine Jr. *Custer Died for Your Sins: An Indian Manifesto*. New York: McMillan, 1969.

Diamond, Neil. "Done Too Soon." Prophet Music, Inc., 1970.

Diamond, Neil. "I Am, I Said." Prophet Music, Inc., 1971.

Dorris Michael. *The Broken Cord*. New York: Harper & Row, 1990.

Douglass, Frederick. *Narrative of the Life of Frederick Douglass*. New York: Dover Thrift, 1995.

Douglass, Frederick. *The Cloud Chamber.* New York: Scribner Paperback Fiction, 1997.

Douglass, Frederick, and Louise Erdrich. *The Crown of Columbus*. New York: Harper-Collins, 1991.

Earling, Debra Magpie. *Perma Red*. New York: Blue Hen Books, 2002.

Ehrlich, Greta. "A fun-filled outrageous collaboration by Erdrich and Dorris." *Chicago Sun Times,* May 5, 1991.

Emecheta, Buchi. *In the Ditch*. Hanover: Walter Heinemann Publishing, 1994.

Erdrich, Louise. *The Antelope Wife*. New York: Harper Perennial, 2009.

Erdrich, Louise. *Baptism of Desire*. New York: Harper & Row, 1989.

Erdrich, Louise. *The Beet Queen*. New York: Henry Holt & Co., 1986.

Erdrich, Louise. *The Bingo Palace*. New York: HarperCollins, 1994.

Erdrich, Louise. *The Birchbark House*. New York: Hyperion, 1999.

Erdrich, Louise. *The Blue Jay's Dance: A Memoir of Early Motherhood*. New York: Harper-Collins, 1995.

Erdrich, Louise. *Books and Islands in Ojibwe Country*. Washington, D.C.: National Geographic Society, 2003.

Erdrich, Louise. *Chickadee*. New York: HarperCollins, 2012.

Erdrich, Louise. *Four Souls*. New York: HarperCollins, 2004.

Erdrich, Louise. *The Game of Silence*. New York: HarperTrophy, 2005.

Erdrich, Louise. *Grandmother's Pigeon*. New York: Hyperion, 1999.

Erdrich, Louise. *Jacklight*. New York: Henry Holt & Co., 1984. Reprint, London: Abacus by Sphere Books, LTD., 1990.

Erdrich, Louise. *The Last Report of the Miracles at Little No Horse*. New York: HarperCollins, 2001.

Erdrich, Louise. *Love Medicine.* New and expanded edition, New York: HarperCollins, 1993.

Erdrich, Louise. (Karen Louise Erdrich). "The Hinterlands." *DART.* Dartmouth Literary Magazine. Vol IV:3, Spring 1976.

Erdrich, Louise. *The Master Butcher's Singing Club.* New York: Harper Collins, 2003.

Erdrich, Louise. "My Kind of Town." *Smithsonian* 37.5, August 2006.

Erdrich, Louise. (Karen Louise Erdrich). "Ode to High School Sex." *DART.* Dartmouth Literary Magazine. Vol IX:1, Fall 1975/Spring 1976.

Erdrich, Louise. *Original Fire.* New York: HarperCollins, 2004.

Erdrich, Louise. *The Painted Drum.* New York: HarperCollins, 2005.

Erdrich, Louise. *The Plague of Doves.* New York: HarperCollins, 2008.

Erdrich, Louise. *The Porcupine Year.* New York: HarperCollins Children's Books, 2008.

Erdrich, Louise. *The Range Eternal.* New York: Hyperion, 2002.

Erdrich, Louise. *The Red Convertible: Selected and New Stories, 1978–2008.* New York: HarperCollins, 2009.

Erdrich, Louise. (Karen Louise Erdrich). "Renny." *DART.* Dartmouth Literary Magazine. Vol III:2, Spring 1975.

Erdrich, Louise. *The Round House.* New York: HarperCollins, 2012.

Erdrich, Louise. *Shadow Tag.* New York: HarperCollins, 2010.

Erdrich, Louise. *Tales of Burning Love.* New York: HarperCollins, 1996.

Erdrich, Louise. *Tracks.* New York: HarperCollins First Perennial Library Ed., 1989.

Equiano, Olaudah. *The Interesting Narrative and Other Writings* Revised Edition. New York: Penguin Classics, 2003.

Ford, John, Dir. *The Searchers.* Los Angeles: Warner Bros., 1956.

Freeman, John. "POETRY: passion still burns brightly in Erdrich's fiery poems." *Minneapolis Star Tribune,* Sept. 7, 2003.

Gates, Henry Louis, Jr. *Faces of America.* PBS Television, Feb. 1—March 3, 2010, www.pbs.org/wnet/facesofamerica/profiles/Louise-erdrich/10/.

Gihring, Tom. "Review: Guthrie's 'Master Butcher's Singing Club Hits Mostly High Notes." *Minnesota Monthly,* Oct. 2010.

Grace, Patricia. *Potiki.* Reprint. Honolulu: University of Hawaii Press, 1995.

Grace, Patricia. *Waiariki.* New York: Penguin, 1987.

Hafen, P. Jane. "Sacramental Language Ritual in the Poetry of Louise Erdrich." *Great Plains Quarterly.* Paper 1101, 1996.

Halliday, Lisa. Interview. "The Art of Fiction No. 208." *Paris Review.* N195, Winter 2010.

Hart, Henry W. *The Ghost Ship.* Crested Butte: Blue Moon Books, 1990.

Hart, Henry W. Email conversation. June 24, 2011.

Hemingway, Ernest. *The Sun Also Rises.* New York: Scribners, 1926 www.historyandthe headlines.abcclio.com

Hogan, Linda. *Calling Myself Home.* Hadley: Greenfield Press, 1978.

Hogan, Linda. *Mean Spirit.* Reprint. New York: Ballantine Books, 1990.

Hogan, Linda. *People of the Whale.* New York: Norton Paperback, 2009.

Hogan, Linda. *Power.* New York: W. W. Norton, 1998.

Hogan, Linda. *Solar Storms.* Reprint. New York: Scribner Paperback Fiction, 1997.

Holm, Tom. Conversation with Frances Washburn. May 9, 2012.

Holm, Tom. *The Great Confusion in Indian Country: Native Americans and Whites in the Progressive Era.* Austin: University of Texas Press, 2005.

Holm, Tom. *The Osage Rose.* Tucson: University of Arizona Press, 2008.

Holm, Tom. *Strong Hearts, Wounded Souls: Native American Veterans of the Vietnam War.* Austin: University of Texas Press, 1996.

Hubbard, Robert. Review: *The Master Butcher's Singing Club. Theater Journal.* Sep 25, 2010. *Project Muse,* http://muse.jhu.edu.

Hufton, Olwen. *The Prospect Before Her: A History of Women in Western Europe, 1500–1800.* New York: Alfred A. Knopf, Inc., 1995.

Hurston, Zora Neale. *Their Eyes Were Watching God.* Reprint. New York: HarperPerennial Modern Classics, 2006.

Hurston, Zora Neale. *Dust Tracks on a Road.* Reprint. New York:First Harper Perennial, 1996.

Ihimaera, Witi. *The Whale Rider.* Auckland: Reed Publishing, 1987.

Jaimes, M. Annette. "The Art of Pandering: A review of The Crown of Columbus." *Wicazo Sa Review,* V9:2, Autumn 1992.

Johnson, E. Pauline, Carole Gerson, and Veronica Strong-Boag, eds. *Tekahionwake: Collected Poems and Selected Prose.* Toronto: University of Toronto Press, 2002.

Jussawalla, Feroza, and Reed Way Dasenbrock, eds. *Interviews with Writers of the Post-Colonial World.* Jackson: University Press of Mississippi, 1992.

Kakutani, Michiko. Book Review. "Books of the Times: Columbus's Diary and Queen Isabella's Jewels." *New York Times,* April 19, 1991.

Kakutani, Michiko. Book Review. "*Antelope Wife:* Myths of Redemption Amid a Legacy of Loss." *The New York Times,* March 24, 1998.

Keenan, Dierdre. "Unrestricted Territory: Gender, Two Spirits, and Louise Erdrich's *The Last Report of the Miracles at Little No Horse. American Indian Culture and Research Journal* 30:2, 2006.

King, Stephen. *The Green Mile.* New York: Scribner, 2003.

King, Stephen. *The Shawshank Redemption.* New York: Warner Books, 1995.

Koeber, Karl, ed. *Traditional Literatures of the American Indian: Texts and Interpretations.* Lincoln: University of Nebraska Press, 1981.

Konigsberg, Eric. "The Last Page." *The New Yorker,* June 16, 1997.

McNickle, D'Arcy, Allen C. Houser, Illus., Alfonso Ortiz. Afterword. *Runner in the Sun.* Reprint. Albuquerque: University of New Mexico Press, 1987.

McNickle, D'Arcy. *The Surrounded.* Reprint. Albuquerque: University of New Mexico Press, 1978.

McNickle, D'Arcy. *Wind From an Enemy Sky.* Reprint. Albuquerque: University of New Mexico Press, 1988.

Miller, Jay. *Mourning Dove: A Salishan Autobiography.* Lincoln: University of Nebraska Press, 1990.

Momaday, N. Scott. *House Made of Dawn.* New York: Harper & Row, 1968.

Morrison, Toni. *Beloved.* New York: Random House, 1997.

Morrison, Toni. *The Bluest Eye.* New York: Holt, Rinehart & Winston, 1970.

Morrison, Toni. *Jazz.* New York: Alfred A. Knopf, 1992.

Morrison, Toni. *Song of Solomon.* New York: Alfred A. Knopf, 1977.

Mourning Dove. *Cogewea, the Half-Blood.* Boston: Four Seas Co., 1927. Reprint First Bison Book Printing. Lincoln: University of Nebraska Press, 1991.

Naipaul, V. S. *A House for Mr. Biswas.* New York: Alfred A. Knopf, 1961.

Ngugi wa thiong'o. *Dreams in the Time of War: A Childhood Memoir.* Reprint. New York: First Anchor Books Edition, 2011.

Ngugi wa thiong'o. *Weep Not, Child.* Hanover: Walter Heinemann Publishers, 1988.

The Norton Anthology of American Literature, Third Ed. New York: W. W. Norton, 1979.

Ojibway Confessions. Tobasonakwuk. Rightojibway.blogspot.com/2011/10/tobasonak wuk-peter-kinew-recieves.html [sic].

Olson, Karen, *The Complicated Life of Louise Erdrich*. barnesandnoble./s/Karen-Olson? keyword=Karen+Olson&Store=allproducts.

Owens, Louis. *Other Destinies: Understanding the American Indian Novel*. Norman: University of Oklahoma Press, 1992.

Parker, Dorothy R. *Singing an Indian Song: A Biography of D'Arcy McNickle*. Lincoln: University of Nebraska Press, 1992.

Reid, E. Shelley. "The Stories We Tell: Louise Erdrich's Identity Narratives." *MELUS*. V25:3/4. Autumn–Winter 2000.

Review of *The Bingo Palace*. *Publishers Weekly*. Jan. 31, 1994.

Review of the stage play, *The Master Butcher's Singing Club*. http:www.variety.com/re view/VE1179436?refCaID=33.

Robinson, Eden. *Monkey Beach*. Reprint. New York: Houghton Mifflin, 2000.

Rybak, Deborah Caulfield, and Jon Tevlin. "Bookmarks: Erdrich Praises Estrogen." *Minneapolis Star Tribune*, Feb. 16, 2003.

Sale, Kirkpatrick. Book Review. "*The Crown of Columbus*, Michael Dorris and Louise Erdrich." *The Nation*, Oct. 21, 1991.

Schechner, Mark. "Erdrichland Suffers A Surfeit of Characters, Plots." *Buffalo News*, April 8, 2001.

Sidhwa, Bapsi. *Cracking India*. Minneapolis: Milkweed Editions, 1991.

Silko, Leslie Marmon. *Ceremony*. New York: Penguin Books, 1977.

Silko, Leslie Marmon. "Book Review of Louise Erdrich's *The Beet Queen*." *Impact: Albuquerque Journal Magazine*. Oct. 7, 1986. Reprint: *Studies in American Indian Literature*. 10:4, Fall 1986.

Silko, Leslie Marmon. *Laguna Women: Poems*. Hadley: Greenfield Press, 1974.

Silko, Leslie Marmon. *The Turquoise Ledge*. New York: Viking Penguin, 2010.

Smith, Wendy. "A Novel Collaboration/Married Authors Compose Their First Written Duet." *Chicago Sun-Times*, May 12, 1991.

Southhampton Writers Conference Press Release, http:www.stonybrook.edu/writers/ writers/reservations.shtml.

Staff Writer. "100 Most Beautiful People." *People Magazine*. May 9, 1990.

Staff Writer. "Wife Claims Dorris was Suicidal for Years, Only She Knew of His Tormented Secret Life." *Seattle Post-Intelligencer*, April 19, 1997.

Stookey, Lorena L. *Louise Erdrich: A Critical Companion*. Westport: Greenwood Press, 1999.

Stratton, Billy J. *Buried in the Shades of Night: Contested Voices, Indian Captivity, and the Legacy of King Philip's War*. Tucson: University of Arizona Press, 2013.

Streitfeld, David. "Writer Was Suspected of Child Abuse: Probe Ends with Michael Dorris Suicide." *The Washington Post*, April 16, 1997.

Tan, Amy. *The Joy Luck Club*. New York: G. P. Putnam's Sons, 1989.

Tan, Amy. *The Kitchen God's Wife*. New York: G. P. Putnam's Sons, 2001.

Tanner, John. *John Tanner, The Falcon*. New York: Perennial, 1994.

Telegraph: Nobel Prize News, www.telegraph.co.uk/news/worldnews/northamerica/ USA/Nobel-literature-prize-judge-Americans-authors-insular-and-ignorant.html.

Tharp, Julie. "Windigo Ways: Eating and Excess in Louise Erdrich's *The Antelope Wife*." *American Indian Culture and Research Journal*. V24:4, 2003.

Tortorello, Michael. "Staging Erdrich." *Minnesota Monthly*, Sept. 1, 2010.

Treuer, David. *The Hiawatha*. New York: Picador, 1999.

Treuer, David. *Little*. New York: Picador, 1995.

Treuer, David. *The Translation of Dr. Appelles: A Love Story*. New York: First Vintage Contemporary Edition, 2006.

Trueheart, Charles. "Marriage for Better or Words." *The Washington Post*, Oct. 19, 1988.

Turtle Mountain Chippewa Indians website, http:/tmbci.net/Wordpress.

Tutuola, Amos. *The Palm Wine Drinkard and My Life in the Bush of Ghosts*. Reprint: New York: Grove Press, 1984.

Umrigar, Thrity. *First Darling of the Morning*. Reprint: New York: Harper Perennial, 2008.

Umrigar, Thrity. *The Space Between Us*. Reprint. New York: First Harper Perennial, 2007.

Wapeton, North Dakota website, www.wahpeton.com

Walker, Alice. *The Color Purple*. New York: Harcourt, Brace, Jovanovich, 1982.

Walker, Alice. *Meridian*. New York: Harcourt, Brace, Jovanovich, 1976.

Walker, Alice. *The Third Life of Grange Copeland*. New York: Harcourt, Brace, Jovanovich, 1970.

Wallis, Velma. *Bird Girl and the Man Who Followed the Sun*. Fairbanks/Seattle: Epicenter Press, 1996.

Wallis, Velma. *Two Old Women*. Fairbanks/Seattle: Epicenter Press, 1993.

Walsh, Dennis. "Catholicism in Louise Erdrich's *Love Medicine* and *Tracks*." *American Indian Culture and Research Journal*, 25:2, 2001.

Washburn, Frances, Shirley Anne Leckie, and Nancy J. Parezo, eds."Zitkala Sa: Bridge Between Two Worlds." In *Their Own Frontier: Women Intellectuals Re-Visioning the American West*. Lincoln: University of Nebraska Press, 2008.

Washburn, Frances. *Elsie's Business*. Lincoln: University of Nebraska Press, 2006.

Washburn, Frances. *The Sacred White Turkey*. Lincoln: University of Nebraska Press, 2010.

Washburn, Frances. *The Red Bird All-Indian Traveling Band*. Tucson: University of Arizona Press, 2014.

Welch, James. *Riding the Earth Boy 40*. Reprint. New York: Penguin, 2004.

Welch, James. *Winter in the Blood*. New York: Harper & Row, 1974.

Williams, Sarah T. "The Three Graces: Louise, Lise, and Heid Erdrich—Sisters First, Writers Second—Look Back on their Parents Hand in Fostering a Shared Love of Language." *Minneapolis Star Tribune*, Feb. 3, 2008.

Wong, Hertha. "Louise Erdrich's *Love Medicine*: Narrative Communities and the Short Story Sequence." In *American Short Story Sequences: Composite and Fictive Communities*, edited by J. Gerald Kenned. Cambridge: University Press, 1995.

Yeats, William Butler. M. L. Rosenthan, ed. "The Second Coming." *Selected Poems and Two Plays of William Butler Yeats*. New York: Collier Books, 1962.

Zepeda, Ofelia. *A Papago Grammar*. Tucson: University of Arizona Press, 1988.

Index

About the Author

FRANCES WASHBURN, PhD, is associate professor and the director of graduate studies in the American Indian Studies Program at the University of Arizona, Tucson, AZ. Washburn is of Lakota/Anishanaabe/Irish/German heritage and grew up on and around Pine Ridge Reservation in South Dakota. Her published works include two novels of American Indian literature, *Elsie's Business* and *The Sacred White Turkey*. A third novel, *The Red Bird All-Indian Traveling Band* has been accepted for publication at the University of Arizona Press.